THE MOST EXPLOSIVE
SCIENCE BOOK
IN THE UNIVERSE
by the Brainwaves

Illustrated by Lisa Swerling and Ralph Lazar

Written by Claire Watts

DK

London, New York, Melbourne,
Munich, and Delhi

Senior Editor Andrea Mills
Senior Art Editor Jim Green
Editor Steven Carton
Designer Katie Knutton

Managing Editor Linda Esposito
Managing Art Editor Diane Thistlethwaite

Consultant Lisa Burke

Publishing Manager Andrew Macintyre
Category Publisher Laura Buller

Production Editor Laragh Kedwell
Senior Production Controller Angela Graef

Jacket Copywriter Adam Powley
Jacket Editor Mariza O'Keeffe

US Editor Margaret Parrish

Look out
for me!

I'm Rocketman and
I'll be whizzing through
these pages, loading up
my backpack with science
stuff and filling my brain
with fantastic facts, ready to
create a special surprise at
the end of the book...

First published in the United States in 2009
by DK Publishing
375 Hudson Street, New York, New York 10014

Copyright © 2009 Dorling Kindersley Limited

09 10 11 12 13 10 9 8 7 6 5 4 3 2 1
BD660—02/09

A catalog record for this book is available
from the Library of Congress.

ISBN: 978-0-75665-152-7

Color reproduction by Media Development and Printing, UK
Printed and bound by Hung Hing, Hong Kong

Discover more at
www.dk.com
www.thebrainwaves.com

CONTENTS

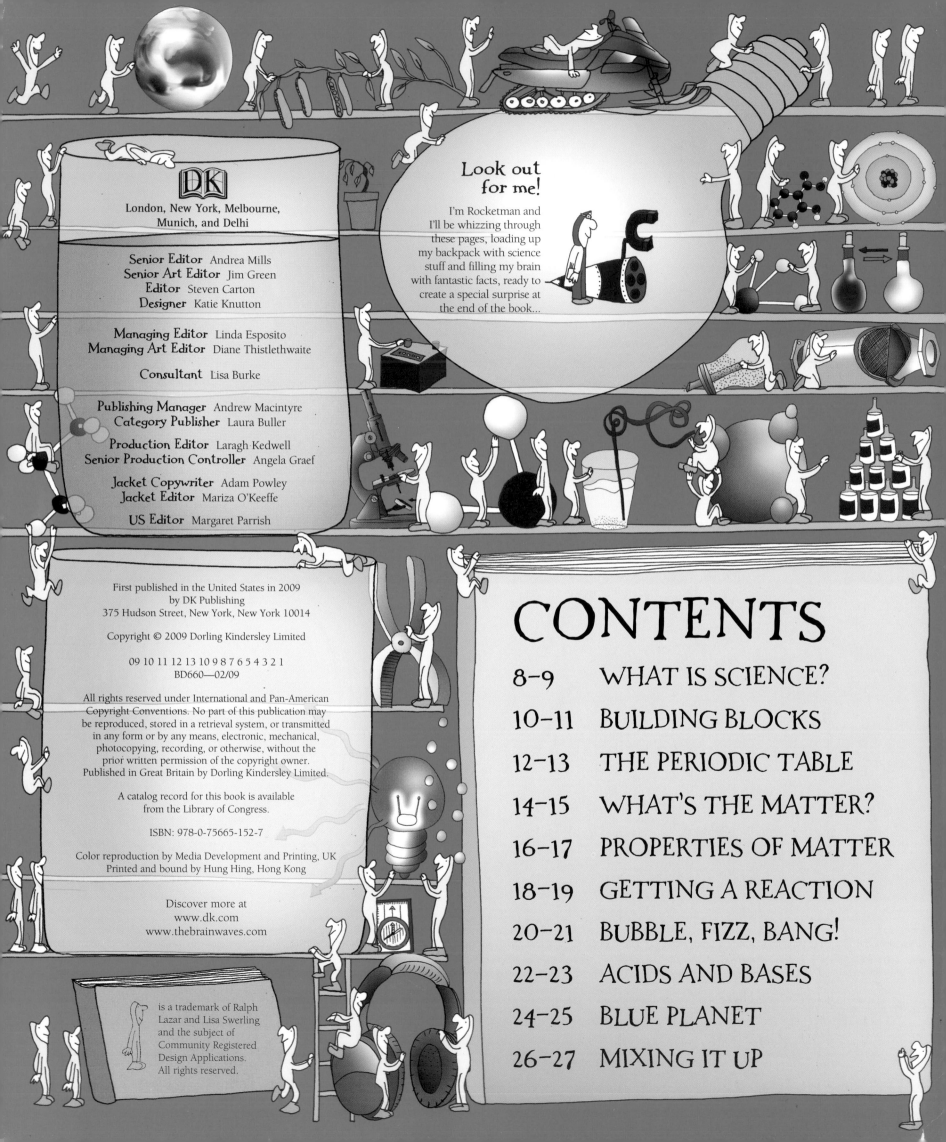

Don't forget us!
Throughout the book, keep your eyes peeled for all of us. We're joining you on this epic journey through the humongous laboratory that is our universe—and we'll be proving that science rocks!

WHAT IS SCIENCE?

From the tiny particles that make us to the vast planets of the universe, science is everywhere. This huge body of information explains and describes the structure, properties, and behavior of all living and nonliving things. However, scientists are still learning. There are questions to be asked, experiments to conduct, and discoveries to be made.

Branches of science

Science is like a big tree, with lots of branches. The three main branches are physics, chemistry, and biology. These split into smaller branches, focusing on a specific field of study. Though science is divided up, all the branches are connected.

This way for the grand science tour!

TOUR STARTS HERE

Physics

The branch of physics concentrates on energy and forces. It includes mechanics, gravity, electricity, and magnetism. Together, physics and chemistry are known as the physical sciences.

An apple a day

Watch your head!

LET'S GET PHYSICAL

Keep your eye on that atom

Go on then—split it!

This is hard work!

How about round wheels?

Nuclear physics

This branch looks at tiny particles called atoms. Nuclear physicists split atoms apart to investigate the nucleus (central part) of the atom.

Mechanics

Motion and the forces that produce it are explained by mechanics, from riding a bicycle to the movement of planets.

Chemistry

The study of the composition of substances and how they react with each other is called chemistry. Chemists split substances to find out what they are made of, and mix them to discover how they behave.

WATCH THE STEP

I'm in the mix!

SCIENTISTS AT WORK

Organic chemistry

This is concerned with substances that contain carbon, vital to living matter. Carbon is also a key component of fossil fuels, medicines, and plastics, so organic chemists often work in the pharmaceutical, petrochemical, and polymer industries.

What shall I do with these plastic bags?

Turn them into fuel!

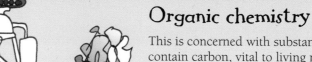

Biology

This natural science looks at the structure and behavior of living organisms, such as plants and animals. Biochemistry, the study of chemical reactions in living things, is a mix of biology and chemistry.

Ant attack!

It's a bug's life!

Don't you know it's rude to stare?

Lovely legs!

PLANTS AND ANIMALS

Zoology and botany

The branch of biology that studies animals is called zoology. The study of plants is called botany. Many cities have zoological and botanical gardens.

Astronomy

The science of stars, planets, and the universe is astronomy. Smaller branches include astrophysics, which studies the structure of objects in space, and cosmology, which focuses on the evolution of the universe.

Roman numerals: MCMLXV + XLIIII =

Arabic numerals: 1965 + 44 = 2009

Mathematics

This branch, studying numbers and shapes, provides the method for measuring and recording observations, and the language used to describe scientific rules.

Inorganic chemistry

Scientists in the branch of inorganic chemistry study substances that contain no carbon or only a very small amount of carbon. They are involved in the production of salts, acids, fertilizers, and ceramics.

Genetics

This branch of biology studies inherited characteristics between generations of plants and animals. Gregor Mendel (1822–84) discovered inheritance by pea plants.

Scientific method

In science, something is only considered a fact if it can be proved. Scientists figure out ways to test ideas and demonstrate conclusively whether they are true or false. This technique of providing proof by testing is called the scientific method.

Hypothesis

Scientists start by thinking up an explanation for something. This is an educated guess, called a hypothesis, based on limited evidence. For example, Benjamin Franklin (1706–90) had a hypothesis that lightning was a form of electricity.

Experiment

Next, a scientific procedure called an experiment is devised to test whether the hypothesis is true or not. The experiment must be conducted several times to prove that the results are accurate.

Observation

The scientist observes what happens, taking measurements where possible. Recording the data is a key part of every science experiment, since it will later form the proof of a scientific fact.

The key on the kite is now electrically charged, so lightning must be a form of electricity

Theory

Testing a hypothesis may lead a scientist to come up with a set of ideas called a theory, intended to explain what happens based on the evidence of the experiment.

Law

The experiment may lead to a new scientific law. A law states what happens in certain circumstances, but it does not explain why it happens. Laws can change as knowledge grows.

BUILDING BLOCKS

For centuries, scientists believed that the very smallest part of any substance was an atom. The word "atom" comes from a Greek word meaning "uncuttable." We now know that atoms are made of smaller particles, and that the number and arrangement of these particles determines whether an atom is oxygen, carbon, gold, or any other substance. An atom cannot be split into its tiny components by any normal physical or chemical means, but it can be split by a nuclear reaction.

Size of an atom

Atoms are so tiny that about six million of them could fit on the period at the end of this sentence.

Inside an atom

Atoms are made up of smaller particles, known as subatomic particles. The quantity of each type of subatomic particle within an atom gives that atom its characteristics. Two of the subatomic particles (protons and electrons) carry electrical charges, but are normally balanced so the atom carries no overall charge.

Niels Bohr

Danish scientist Niels Bohr (1885–1962) came up with the idea of electrons moving in distinct shells around an atom's nucleus, just like moons orbiting a planet.

Electrons whizz around the nucleus in regions called electron orbits—each one contains a limited number of electrons, but atoms may have up to seven different orbits

Electrons have a negative electrical charge (–)

Most of the particles that make up the atom are found in the central part of the atom, called the nucleus

Protons have a positive electrical charge (+)

Neutrons have no electrical charge, and are held to protons by special forces in the nucleus

There is so much empty space in the atom that if the electrons were orbiting around a football stadium, the nucleus would be a pea at the center of the field, with the rest of the space unused

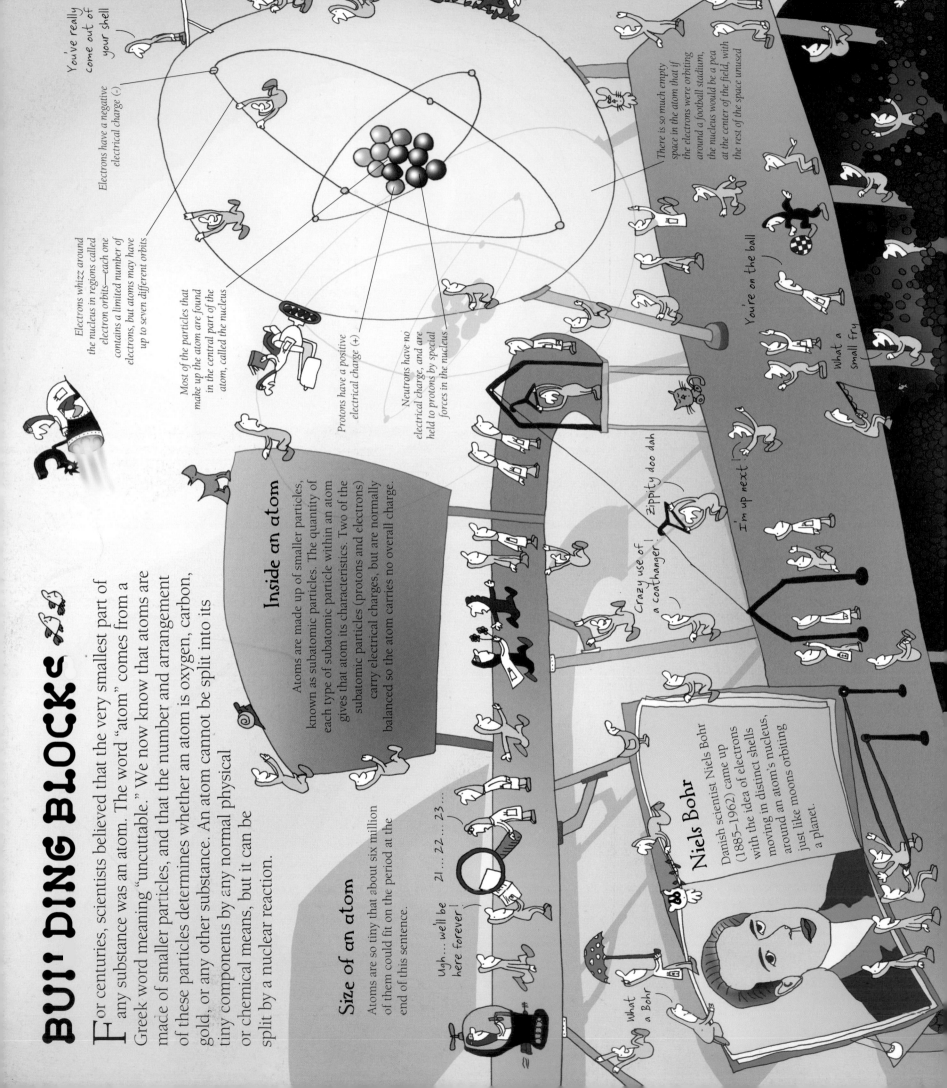

You've really come out of your shell

Ugh... we'll be here forever!

21 ... 22 ... 23 ...

What a Bohr

Zippity doo dah

Crazy use of a coathanger!

I'm up next

You're on the ball

What a small fry

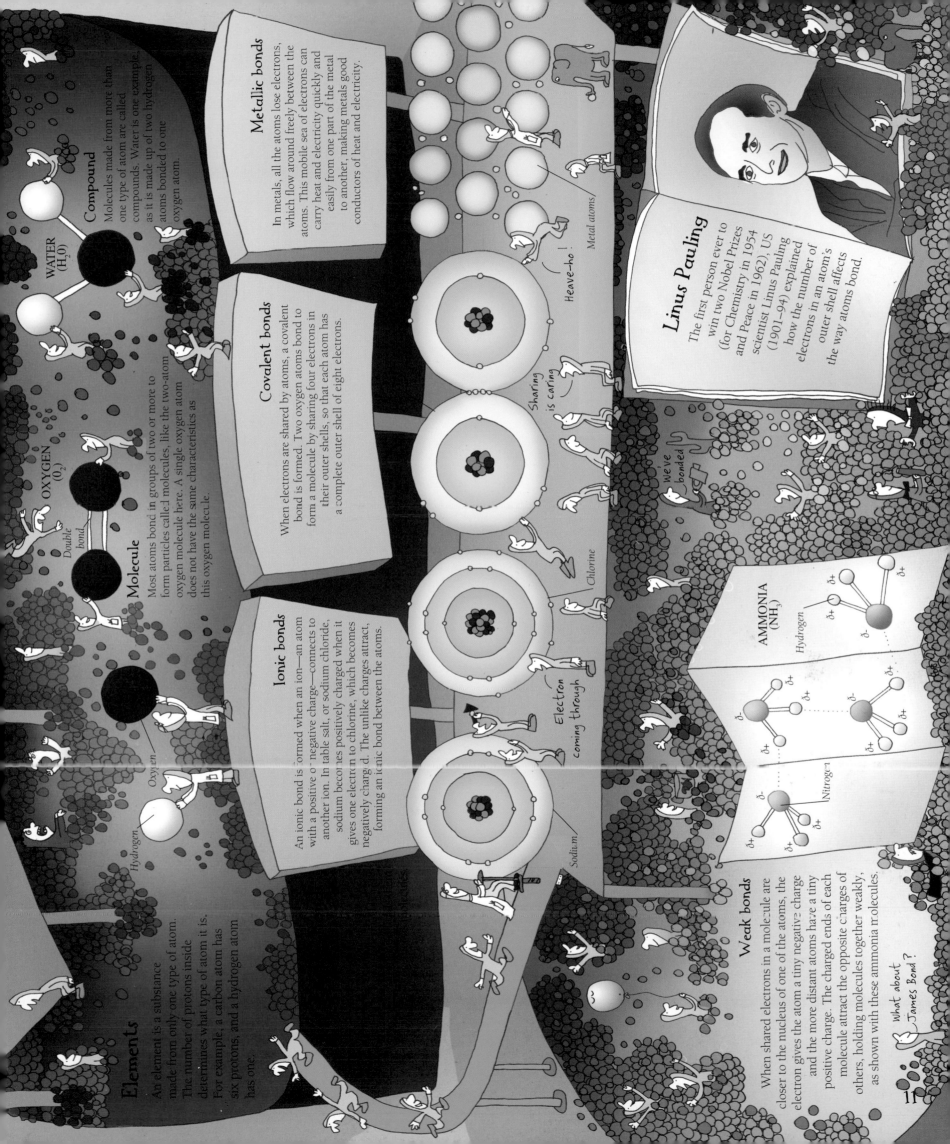

Compound

Molecules made from more than one type of atom are called compounds. Water is one example, as it is made up of two hydrogen atoms bonded to one oxygen atom.

WATER (H₂O)

Double bond

Molecule

Most atoms bond in groups of two or more to form particles called molecules, like the two-atom oxygen molecule here. A single oxygen atom does not have the same characteristics as this oxygen molecule.

OXYGEN (O₂)

Elements

An element is a substance made from only one type of atom. The number of protons inside determines what type of atom it is. For example, a carbon atom has six protons, and a hydrogen atom has one.

Hydrogen

Oxygen

Metallic bonds

In metals, all the atoms lose electrons, which flow around freely between the atoms. This mobile sea of electrons can carry heat and electricity quickly and easily from one part of the metal to another, making metals good conductors of heat and electricity.

Metal atoms

Heave-ho!

Covalent bonds

When electrons are shared by atoms, a covalent bond is formed. Two oxygen atoms bond to form a molecule by sharing four electrons in their outer shells, so that each atom has a complete outer shell of eight electrons.

Sharing is caring

Chlorine

Ionic bonds

An ionic bond is formed when an ion—an atom with a positive or negative charge—connects to another ion. In table salt, or sodium chloride, sodium becomes positively charged when it gives one electron to chlorine, which becomes negatively charged. The unlike charges attract, forming an ionic bond between the atoms.

Electron coming through

Sodium

Linus Pauling

The first person ever to win two Nobel Prizes (for Chemistry in 1954 and Peace in 1962). US scientist Linus Pauling (1901–94) explained how the number of electrons in an atom's outer shell affects the way atoms bond.

We've bonded

AMMONIA (NH₃)

Hydrogen

Nitrogen

Weak bonds

When shared electrons in a molecule are closer to the nucleus of one of the atoms, the electron gives the atom a tiny negative charge and the more distant atoms have a tiny positive charge. The charged ends of each molecule attract the opposite charges of others, holding molecules together weakly, as shown with these ammonia molecules.

What about James Bond?

11

THE PERIODIC TABLE

Every element that we know about in the universe is set out in order of the increasing size of its atoms on the periodic table. The elements are arranged in rows and columns that reveal repeating patterns in their structure and properties. Most of these elements exist naturally in the universe, but some are created artificially. The rows across are called periods and the columns are called groups.

Reading the table

Each element has an atomic number, a symbol, and an atomic mass. This box shows the element germanium, a light gray metal.

Atomic number (32)
The number of protons in the atom's nucleus is shown by the atomic number at the top. Elements are sometimes called by this number.

32
Ge
Germanium
73

Chemical symbol (Ge)
Above the element's name is a chemical symbol used to represent the element in chemical equations.

Atomic mass (73)
The number of protons and neutrons in the nucleus is shown by the atomic mass at the bottom.

How the table is arranged

Starting with hydrogen, elements are arranged by atomic number and continue across the rows. Atomic mass usually increases with atomic number, so most elements at the start of the table are light and most at the end are heavy.

Period (rows)

Each row corresponds with the number of electron orbits (also called shells) its atoms have. So, hydrogen in row 1 has one shell, while gold in row 6 has six shells.

Group (columns)

Most elements in a group have the same number of electrons in their outer orbits. Elements become less reactive across the rows, so group 1 elements catch fire in oxygen, while group 18 elements are unreactive gases.

I'm top of the table

Hydrogen
Element 1 is colorless and odorless, and makes up 88 percent of all the atoms in the universe.

Sodium
This soft metal can be cut with a knife, but it explodes if it comes into contact with water.

Silicon
Some people think alien life might be based on silicon, which has similar properties to carbon, the basis of all life on Earth.

Stop!!!

1 2 3 4 5 6 7 8 9

	1	2	3	4	5	6	7	8	9
1	1 H Hydrogen 1								
2	3 Li Lithium 7	4 Be Beryllium 9							
3	11 Na Sodium 23	12 Mg Magnesium 24							
4	19 K Potassium 39	20 Ca Calcium 40	21 Sc Scandium 45	22 Ti Titanium 48	23 V Vanadium 51	24 Cr Chromium 52	25 Mg Manganese 55	26 Fe Iron 56	27 Co Cobalt 59
5	37 Rb Rubidium 85	38 Sr Strontium 88	39 Y Yttrium 89	40 Zr Zirconium 91	41 Nb Niobium 93	42 Mo Molybdenum 96	43 Tc Technetium 98	44 Ru Ruthenium 101	45 Rh Rhodium 103
6	55 Cs Cesium 133	56 Ba Barium 137	57 – 71 (see below)	72 Hf Hafnium 178	73 Ta Tantalum 181	74 W Tungsten 184	75 Re Rhenium 186	76 Os Osmium 190	77 Ir Iridium 192
7	87 Fr Francium 223	88 Ra Radium 226	89 – 103 (see below)	104 Rf Rutherfordium 261	105 Db Dubnium 262	106 Sg Seaborgium 266	107 Bh Bohrium 264	108 Hs Hassium 277	109 Mt Meitnerium 268

Look, no hands!

Mendeleyev

When Russian chemist Dmitri Mendeleyev (1834–1907) devised the periodic table in 1869, it was so accurate that he even left gaps in the right places for elements that were not yet discovered.

we're not worthy

It's elementary

57 La Lanthanum 139	58 Ce Cerium 140	59 Pr Praseodymium 141	60 Nd Neodymium 144	61 Pm Promethium 145	62 Sm Samarium 150
89 Ac Actinium 227	90 Th Thorium 232	91 Pa Protactinium 231	92 U Uranium 238	93 Np Neptunium 237	94 Pu Plutonium 244

Uranium
Radioactive element 92 is used as a fuel in nuclear power plants.

we have chemistry

Help me, Helium Man!

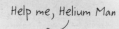
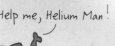

The coinage metals

Copper
Pots and pans are made of copper, because it spreads heat well.

Silver
Cutlery and other utensils are sometimes made of silver.

Gold
Easy to shape, gold is perfect for coins and jewelry.

Key

The elements can be divided into categories with similar properties, such as appearance or behavior. Each element on the periodic table is color-coded to match one of the categories in this key.

That's a gas

Nitrogen
Vital for building cells in all living things, nitrogen is used in fertilizer to help crops grow.

Uplifting

Carbon
Element 6 exists in many forms, from black soot to sparkling diamonds.

Phosphorus
Highly reactive, phosphorus glows bright green in the dark, and comes in differently colored forms.

Helium
Lighter than air, helium is used to fill balloons and airships, making them float.

Aluminum
Earth's most common metal is used to make aircraft and soda cans.

Like a dip?

Chlorine
Yellow-green element 17 is used to kill bacteria in swimming pools and drinking water supplies.

Where is element 117?

Alkali metals
Silvery solids at room temperature, alkali metals are good conductors of heat and electricity.

Alkaline Earth metals
These elements combine with many elements in the Earth's crust to form stable compounds.

Transition metals
Generally hard, tough, and shiny at room temperature, these metals have high melting points.

Lanthanoids
These silvery reactive metals occur only as compounds in nature and are hard to separate.

Actinoids
Dangerously radioactive metals, actinoids are usually created synthetically.

Poor metals
These are similar to transition metals, but fairly soft and with low melting and boiling points.

Nonmetals
Poor conductors of electricity and heat, nonmetals melt at low temperatures.

Noble gases
These elements do not combine readily with others, and are gases at room temperature.

Hydrogen
The simplest and lightest of all the elements, hydrogen does not fit into any category.

10	11	12	13	14	15	16	17	18

								2 He Helium 1
			5 B Boron 11	6 C Carbon 12	7 N Nitrogen 14	8 O Oxygen 16	9 F Fluorine 19	10 Ne Neon 20
			13 Al Aluminum 27	14 Si Silicon 28	15 P Phosphorus 31	16 S Sulfur 32	17 Cl Chlorine 35	18 Ar Argon 40
28 Ni Nickel 59	29 Cu Copper 64	30 Zn Zinc 65	31 Ga Gallium 70	32 Ge Germanium 73	33 As Arsenic 75	34 Se Selenium 79	35 Br Bromine 80	36 Kr Krypton 84
46 Pd Palladium 103	47 Ag Silver 108	48 Cd Cadmium 112	49 In Indium 115	50 Sn Tin 119	51 Sb Antimony 122	52 Te Tellurium 128	53 I Iodine 127	54 Xe Xenon 131
78 Pt Platinum 192	79 Au Gold 197	80 Hg Mercury 201	81 Tl Thallium 204	82 Pb Lead 207	83 Bi Bismuth 209	84 Po Polonium 209	85 At Astatine 210	86 Rn Radon 222
110 Ds Darmstadium 271	111 Rg Roentgenium 272	112 Uub Ununbium 285	113 Uut Ununtrium 284	114 Uuq Ununquadium 289	115 Uup Ununpentium 288	116 Uuh Ununhexium 292		118 Uuo Ununoctium 294

Mad hatter

Mercury
A liquid metal at room temperature, mercury was used in hat-making, until it was discovered that it made people insane!

I'm in my element

63 Eu Europium 152	64 Gd Gadolinium 157	65 Tb Terium 159	66 Dy Dysprosium 163	67 Ho Holmium 165	68 Er Erbium 167	69 Tm Thulium 169	70 Yb Ytterbium 173	71 Lu Lutetium 175
95 Am Americium 243	96 Cm Curium 247	97 Bk Berkelium 247	98 Cf Californium 251	99 Es Einsteinium 252	100 Fm Fermium 257	101 Md Mendelevium 258	102 No Nobelium 259	103 Lr Lawrencium 262

Synthetic elements
All the elements heavier than plutonium are made artificially, or synthesized. Elements 112–118 have temporary names because they have been recently synthesized, but element 117—called ununseptium—has not yet been synthesized, and is missing from the table.

Slow down

Natural elements
All matter on Earth is made up of one or more of 94 elements that occur naturally. Some of these elements, such as technetium, are produced when radioactive natural elements disintegrate.

Einsteinium
Named after Albert Einstein, this element is produced from plutonium in a nuclear process that takes several years.

Are you my daddy?

WHAT'S THE MATTER?

Everything in the universe that is made up of atoms and occupies space is called matter. It is everywhere, in all the animals, objects, and substances that you can see and touch, and in the stars and planets far out in space. Matter is even in the things you can't see, floating around as invisible gases in the air, and as tiny, drifting particles that your nose detects as smells.

Types of matter

Matter is divided into two types: living and nonliving matter. Your body is composed of living matter, while objects, such as a metal spoon, are composed of nonliving matter.

We matter, too!

Giddy up!

Woof!

States of matter

Matter exists in different states, depending on how much energy it contains. The most common states of matter are solid, liquid, and gas. Sometimes matter exists in other states, such as plasmas, which are gases made from parts of atoms.

Solid

Molecules in a solid have less energy than those in a liquid or gas. They can vibrate but cannot move around. Solids have a fixed volume, which means they take up a fixed amount of space, and most have a definite shape.

Not much space between molecules in solids

Do you have orange sauce flavor?

Brrrr!

FREEZING

MELTING

Changing states

Matter can change from one state to another by adding or removing energy. For example, water can change from a liquid to solid ice or to a gas, steam. The molecules within ice, water, and steam are identical but they move in different ways.

Quack!

Cool

Heating

Heating a substance gives it more energy, so its molecules move faster and farther apart. Heating a solid melts it into a liquid, and heating a liquid evaporates it into a gas.

It's melting!

Lucky duck

Cooling

Cooling a substance takes away energy, making its molecules slow down and move closer together. Cooling a gas condenses it into a liquid, and cooling a liquid freezes it into a solid.

Liquid

Molecules in a liquid have more energy, so they move faster and spread out farther from each other. Liquids have a fixed volume, but no definite shape.

Molecules are evenly spread out in liquids

EVAPORATION

This is easy

Living matter

From microscopic organisms to humans, animals, and plants, all living things are composed of living matter. This type of matter can move, grow on its own, and reproduce.

Nonliving matter

Everything that is not alive, such as rocks, metals, water, and air, is made up of nonliving matter. This matter cannot move by itself, grow, or reproduce.

Nonmatter

Some things, such as light, heat, and sound, are not made of atoms and do not take up space. These things are not matter but forms of energy. Everything that exists is composed either of matter or of energy.

Sublimation

Most substances have to go through a liquid state to turn from a solid to a gas and back. However, some substances, such as carbon dioxide (CO_2), can change directly from gas to solid and back in a process called sublimation.

Pressure

Changes in pressure can make matter change state, too. Increasing pressure forces molecules together, which has the same effect as cooling. Decreasing pressure allows molecules to spread out, which has the same effect as heating.

Gas

Gas molecules have the most energy, so they move fastest and spread out the farthest. A gas has no definite volume or shape. It spreads to fit the area that contains it, and if it is placed in an open container, it will flow out and mix with the surrounding air.

Solid carbon dioxide (CO_2) is known as dry ice

15

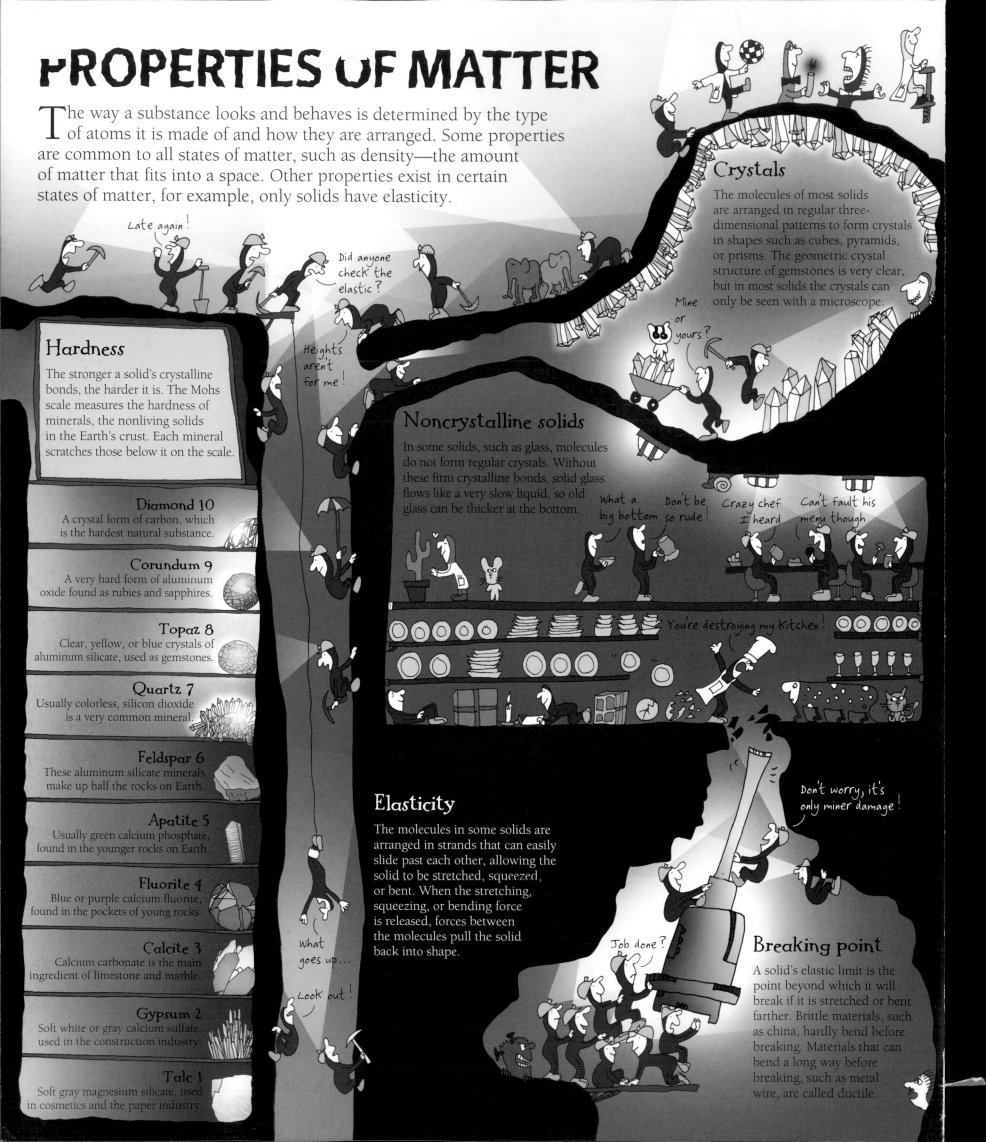

PROPERTIES OF MATTER

The way a substance looks and behaves is determined by the type of atoms it is made of and how they are arranged. Some properties are common to all states of matter, such as density—the amount of matter that fits into a space. Other properties exist in certain states of matter, for example, only solids have elasticity.

Hardness

The stronger a solid's crystalline bonds, the harder it is. The Mohs scale measures the hardness of minerals, the nonliving solids in the Earth's crust. Each mineral scratches those below it on the scale.

Diamond 10
A crystal form of carbon, which is the hardest natural substance.

Corundum 9
A very hard form of aluminum oxide found as rubies and sapphires.

Topaz 8
Clear, yellow, or blue crystals of aluminum silicate, used as gemstones.

Quartz 7
Usually colorless, silicon dioxide is a very common mineral.

Feldspar 6
These aluminum silicate minerals make up half the rocks on Earth.

Apatite 5
Usually green calcium phosphate, found in the younger rocks on Earth.

Fluorite 4
Blue or purple calcium fluorite, found in the pockets of young rocks.

Calcite 3
Calcium carbonate is the main ingredient of limestone and marble.

Gypsum 2
Soft white or gray calcium sulfate, used in the construction industry.

Talc 1
Soft gray magnesium silicate, used in cosmetics and the paper industry.

Crystals

The molecules of most solids are arranged in regular three-dimensional patterns to form crystals in shapes such as cubes, pyramids, or prisms. The geometric crystal structure of gemstones is very clear, but in most solids the crystals can only be seen with a microscope.

Noncrystalline solids

In some solids, such as glass, molecules do not form regular crystals. Without these firm crystalline bonds, solid glass flows like a very slow liquid, so old glass can be thicker at the bottom.

Elasticity

The molecules in some solids are arranged in strands that can easily slide past each other, allowing the solid to be stretched, squeezed, or bent. When the stretching, squeezing, or bending force is released, forces between the molecules pull the solid back into shape.

Breaking point

A solid's elastic limit is the point beyond which it will break if it is stretched or bent farther. Brittle materials, such as china, hardly bend before breaking. Materials that can bend a long way before breaking, such as metal wire, are called ductile.

Viscosity

The way the molecules of a fluid rub against each other affects how easily it will flow. Fluids that resist flowing, such as ketchup, are called viscous, while fluids that flow easily, such as water, have low viscosity.

Surface tension

Molecules at the surface of a liquid are attracted downward by the liquid molecules below, forming an invisible, elastic skin. This effect, called surface tension, enables tiny insects, such as water striders, to walk on water.

Meniscus

Liquids have a curved surface, called the meniscus, caused by the variation in surface tension where the liquid touches the container. Water molecules are more attracted to the container than to each other, so water's meniscus curves up. But mercury molecules are strongly attracted to each other, so the meniscus curves down.

Expansion

When matter is heated, the molecules move farther apart, so the substance expands. As the gas in a hot air balloon is heated, it expands, making the balloon swell. The air inside the balloon is less dense than the air outside, so the balloon rises.

Compression

Gas molecules can be compressed to fit into a smaller space. When the pressure is released, the gas expands with great force. Gas dissolved in a liquid under pressure expands into bubbles of fizz when the container is opened, relieving the pressure.

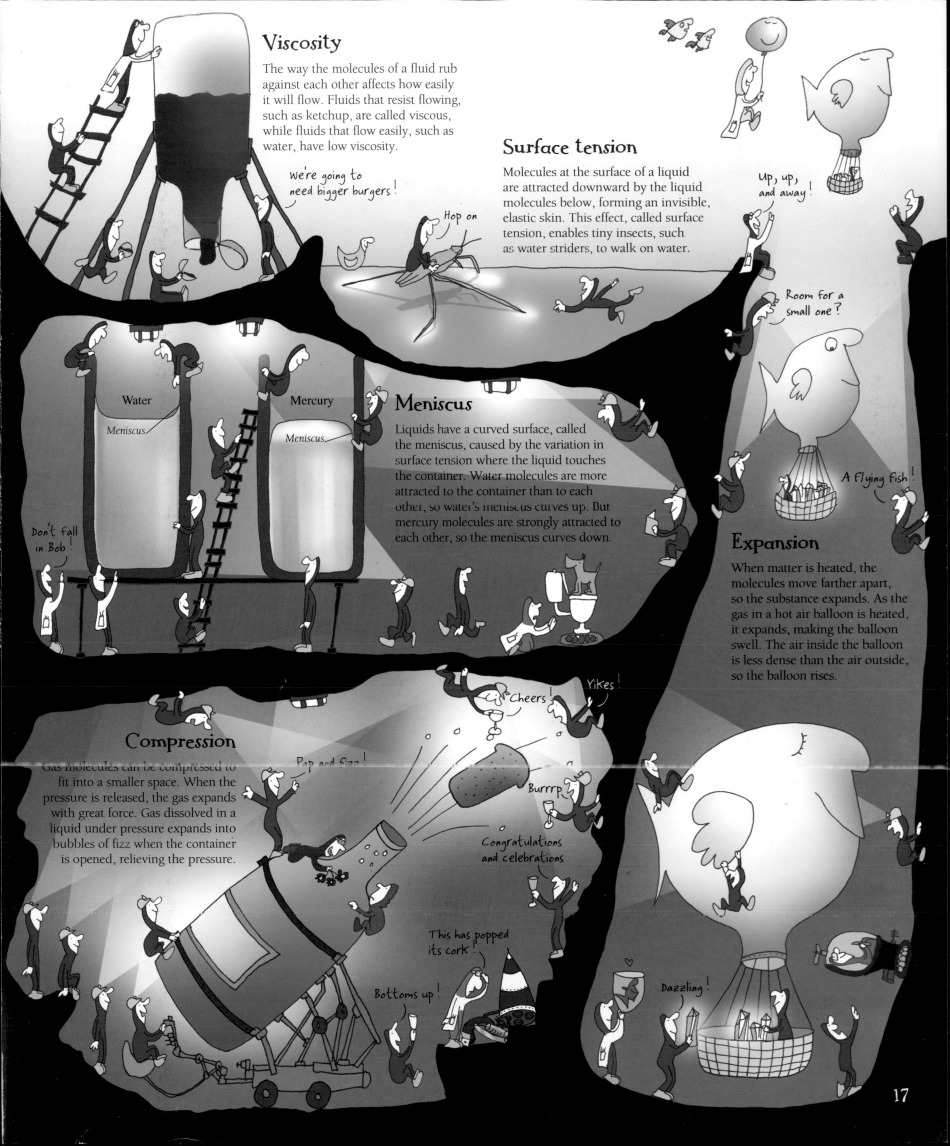

GETTING A REACTION

Chemical reactions are happening all the time, all around us, and even inside our bodies, as molecules split apart and join together to make new molecules. The substances that are changed by a chemical reaction are called reactants, while the substances that exist after the reaction are called products. Some chemical reactions can split a molecule into a pure element, but they cannot split an atom—that requires a nuclear reaction.

Chemical change

When substances undergo chemical changes, the molecules within them are rearranged to form new substances. One example is when iron is exposed to air. Iron atoms combine with oxygen atoms to form molecules of iron oxide or rust.

Physical change

Chopping, cutting, and crushing changes the way a substance looks, but does not change the molecules that make up the substance. These are physical changes, not chemical changes.

Nonreversible reaction

In most chemical reactions, it is impossible to change the products back into the reactants. Burning a product makes it react with oxygen in the air to create smoke and ash, which can never be turned back into the original material.

Reversible reaction

Some chemical reactions can be reversed. The forward reaction changes the reactants into products and the backward reaction changes the products back to reactants.

How a chemical reaction works

During a chemical reaction, the bonds that hold atoms together as molecules are broken apart and new bonds are made, forming new molecules. The atoms themselves do not change.

Carbon

PROPANE

Hydrogen

OXYGEN

+

(BURNING) →

CARBON DIOXIDE + WATER

Hydrogen

Oxygen

Oxygen Carbon

Burning propane

When propane gas burns, its carbon and hydrogen molecules combine with oxygen molecules in the air. Carbon and some of the oxygen atoms form carbon dioxide molecules, while hydrogen and the other oxygen atoms form water molecules.

Perfect balance

Water molecules contain two hydrogen and one oxygen

Hydrogen molecule contains two hydrogen atoms

Oxygen molecule contains two oxygen atoms

Balancing act

A chemical reaction does not create or destroy atoms. It rearranges them, so all the atoms in a reaction's products still exist in the reactants. In this reaction, two hydrogen molecules (four atoms) and one oxygen molecule (two atoms) are rearranged to make two water molecules (four hydrogen and two oxygen atoms).

What a gas!

Tastes like chicken!

A toast to change!

Just add a pincer salt!

You guys used to hang out, remember?

Who is this pond scum!

Are you paying?

I'm stuffed!

Chemical equations

A chemical equation is a mathematical way to show what happens in a chemical reaction. Chemical symbols are used in place of the names of substances. There must be equal quantities of each atom on both sides of the equation to show that the same atoms exist before and after the reaction.

HYDROGEN + OXYGEN → WATER

$$2H_2 + O_2 \rightarrow 2H_2O$$

There are two of these molecules

This molecule is made of two hydrogen atoms

This molecule is made of two oxygen atoms

There are two of these molecules

This molecule contains two hydrogen atoms and one oxygen atom

Hope we get a tip

Here's our very heavy specials board

Wish they'd change our uniform…

Orange was never your color

These crumbs are simply divine!

Here goes the diet!

19

BUBBLE, FIZZ, BANG!

Slow reactions, like rusting, take place over months or even years, so you can't see them happening. Other reactions are much faster and more dramatic, releasing bubbles of gas, a glow of light, or a sudden explosion. Chemical energy holds molecules together and energy is also needed to break them, so whenever a chemical reaction occurs, energy is used or released.

Reaction rates

When moving molecules collide with each other, reactions happen. If these molecules are moving slowly, there are few collisions and the reaction is slow, but faster molecules mean more collisions and quick reactions.

Temperature

Warm molecules move fast and collide more, so raising the temperature speeds up reactions and lowering the temperature slows them down. Keeping food cool slows down the reactions that would make it go bad.

Concentration

The more molecules there are to react, the faster the reaction will be. Concentrated solutions contain many reactant molecules, so they react more quickly than weaker ones. A concentrated dye colors cloth faster than a weaker one.

Light

Some chemical reactions need light energy to make them work. The chemicals used on photographic film react when they are exposed to light to produce an image. Without light, the film remains blank.

Catalyst

Substances that speed up chemical reactions but do not change themselves are called catalysts. Cars are equipped with catalytic converters, which use a catalyst to help convert harmful exhaust gases, such as nitrogen oxide, carbon monoxide, and hydrocarbons, into less polluting substances.

Nitrogen oxide (NO)

Hydrocarbon

Catalyst made of platinum and rhodium metals

Carbon monoxide (CO)

CATALYTIC CONVERTER

Exhaust gases from car's engine enter the converter

Reactions in the converter produce less harmful substances

Water (H_2O)

Carbon dioxide (CO_2)

Nitrogen (N_2)

Splitting

Some reactions split molecules to form simpler molecules or elements. Iron is found naturally in compounds called iron ores. The ore is heated in a process called smelting to break the chemical bonds and obtain pure iron.

Iron ore + Carbon $\rightarrow$ Iron + Carbon dioxide

$$2Fe_2O_3 + 3C \rightarrow 4Fe + 3CO_2$$

Joining

Some reactions join elements or molecules together to form new, more complex molecules. When iron ore is smelted, the carbon in the fuel reacts with the oxygen in the iron ore to produce carbon dioxide.

Heavy metal man!

Swapping

In displacement reactions, metal in a compound swaps with another metal. When copper is placed in clear silver nitrate solution, some copper swaps places with some silver, coating the metal silver and turning the liquid blue.

Bring on the bling

He's so demanding

Copper + Silver nitrate $\rightarrow$ Copper nitrate + Silver

$$Cu + 2AgNO_3 \rightarrow Cu(NO_3)_2 + 2Ag$$

Copper in clear silver nitrate

Copper turns silver and liquid is blue

Rock on

I'm instrumental in the success of the band

Energetic performance!

Energy levels

Some chemical reactions use up more energy by breaking bonds than they release by creating new bonds. Other reactions produce energy because they use less energy to break bonds and release more by creating bonds.

Endothermic reactions

Chemical reactions that use up energy in order to work are called endothermic. When the substances in an instant cool pack mix together, an endothermic reaction results, absorbing heat from the person the pack is touching and cooling them down.

This will help you cool off

Exothermic reactions

Reactions that release a lot of energy in the form of heat, light, and noise are called exothermic reactions. Explosions are exothermic reactions that release a huge amount of energy in a sudden, fierce burst.

Ooooh yeah

What a set!

More! More!

ACIDS AND BASES

The tangy taste of a lemon and the sharp sting of a nettle are the result of chemical substances called acids. However, these are mild examples. Strong acids can burn flesh and dissolve metal. The chemical opposite of an acid is called a base. Cleaning products and medicines are often bases. They feel slippery and soapy, but strong ones can also be corrosive.

Acids

When some compounds dissolve in water, they produce hydrogen ions (H^+) that have lost their electron and become positively charged. These solutions are called acids.

Bases

When some substances dissolve in water, negatively charged hydroxide ions (OH^-) are created. These substances are called bases and their solutions are alkalis. All bases react with acids to form salts.

pH scale

Acidity is measured on the pH scale. The pH stands for "power of the hydrogen" because acidity levels depend on the concentration of hydrogen ions. Substances below 7 are acidic, and those above 7 are alkaline.

Indicators

Chemicals used to test whether a substance is acid or alkaline are called indicators. Some produce a red color for acid and blue for alkali. Universal indicator paper (also called litmus paper) produces a range of colors indicating where the solution fits in the pH scale.

SPECIAL OFFER—EVERY LEMON MUST GO

SOAP OF THE CENTURY!

Cheep! Cheep! Very cheap!

You're such a lemon!

He just got paid

SUPERMARKET

Bring on the bargains!

That's a good indication...

INDICATORS

It's a must-have!

pH7
Pure water has a neutral pH of 7—neither acid nor alkali.

NEUTRAL

pH6
Fresh milk is very slightly acidic, but when it gets old, the acidity increases so it tastes sour.

MILK

Monster in the milk aisle!

pH5
Bananas are much less acidic than citrus fruit such as lemons and oranges.

Shop 'til you drop!

pH3
Lemon juice is so acidic that it can wear away the tough enamel of the teeth.

pH4
Canned tomatoes are slightly more acidic than fresh ones.

pH1
Car batteries contain strong sulfuric acid.

HIGHLY ACIDIC

Hydrochloric acid is offer of the week!

pH2
Hydrochloric acid is produced naturally in the stomach to help the digestion of food.

Haven't you had a gut-full?

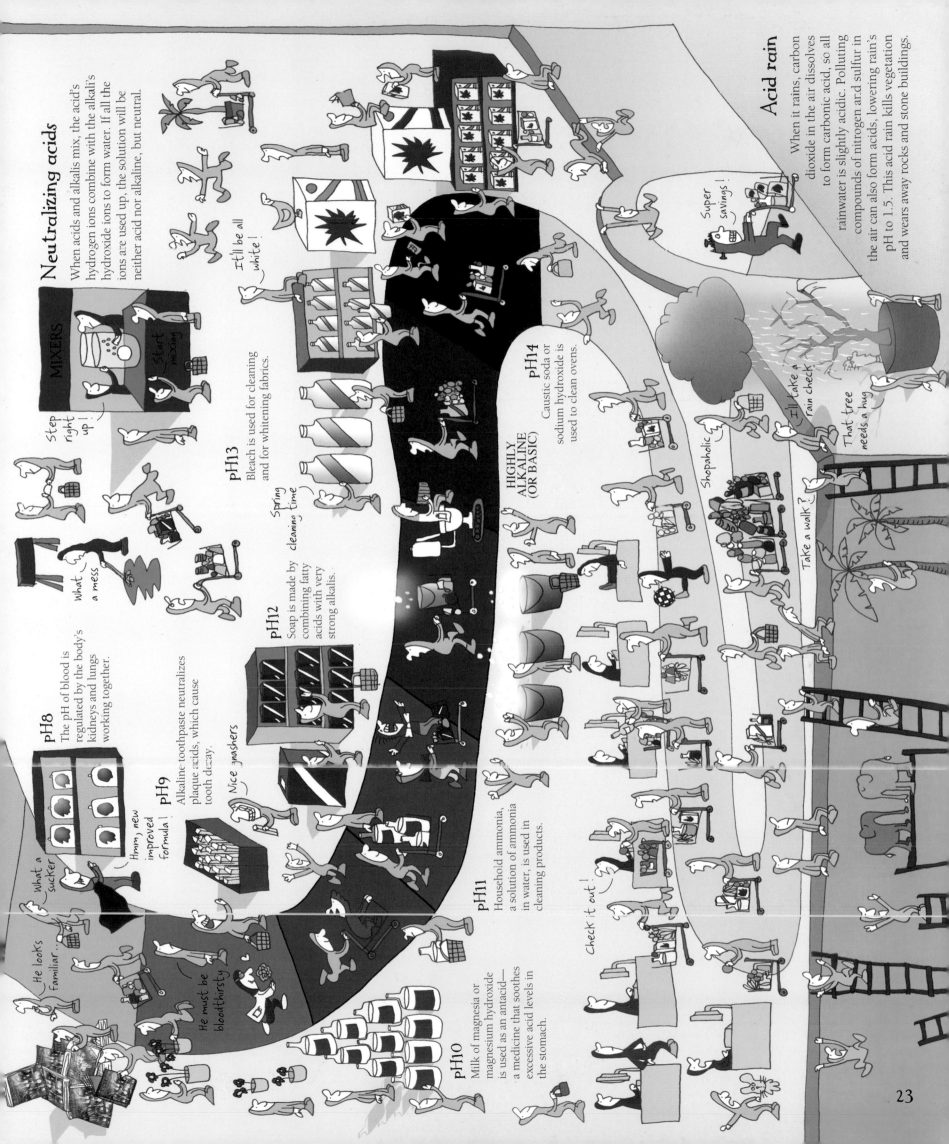

Neutralizing acids

When acids and alkalis mix, the acid's hydrogen ions combine with the alkali's hydroxide ions to form water. If all the ions are used up, the solution will be neither acid nor alkaline, but neutral.

MIXERS

Start mixing

Step right up!

It'll be all white!

pH13
Bleach is used for cleaning and for whitening fabrics.

Spring cleaning time

pH12
Soap is made by combining fatty acids with very strong alkalis.

Nice gnashers

pH8
The pH of blood is regulated by the body's kidneys and lungs working together.

pH9
Alkaline toothpaste neutralizes plaque acids, which cause tooth decay.

What a mess

Hmm, new improved formula!

What a sucker

He looks familiar...

He must be bloodthirsty

pH10
Milk of magnesia or magnesium hydroxide is used as an antacid—a medicine that soothes excessive acid levels in the stomach.

pH11
Household ammonia, a solution of ammonia in water, is used in cleaning products.

Check it out!

HIGHLY ALKALINE (OR BASIC)

pH14
Caustic soda or sodium hydroxide is used to clean ovens.

Super savings!

Shopaholic

Take a walk?

I'll take a rain check

That tree needs a hug

Acid rain

When it rains, carbon dioxide in the air dissolves to form carbonic acid, so all rainwater is slightly acidic. Polluting compounds of nitrogen and sulfur in the air can also form acids, lowering rain's pH to 1.5. This acid rain kills vegetation and wears away rocks and stone buildings.

23

BLUE PLANET

Water is the most common compound on Earth. A water molecule is made up of one oxygen atom bonded to two hydrogen atoms in such a way that it can stick together or stick to other things. This unusual structure makes water very useful. It is the only compound in the world to exist naturally in all three states of matter: as solid ice and snow, as liquid water, and as a gas in the atmosphere.

Water

Molecules of a similar size to water molecules boil to form gases well below zero. However, water stays a liquid until it reaches 212°F (100°C). Extra heat is needed to break the hydrogen bonds that hold water molecules together and allow them to float away as a gas.

Molecular structure

In a water molecule, the oxygen atom has a slightly negative electrical charge and the hydrogen atoms have slightly positive electrical charges. Oxygen atoms in one water molecule attract hydrogen atoms in another water molecule, holding many molecules together.

Hydrogen bond between molecules

Oxygen

Hydrogen

δ+

δ- (negative charge)

Molecular bond

δ+ (positive charge)

Ice

At 32°F (0°C), water freezes into ice. In most substances, freezing draws molecules together, but as water freezes, its molecules move apart to form crystals. This makes water expand by about 10 percent. As a result, ice is less dense than water, which is why it floats.

Molecules form a rigid crystalline shape

Steam

Water boils at 212°F (100°C) to produce a gas called steam. As the temperature drops, the hydrogen bonds pull the water molecules back together to form a cloud of tiny water droplets, called water vapor, suspended in the air.

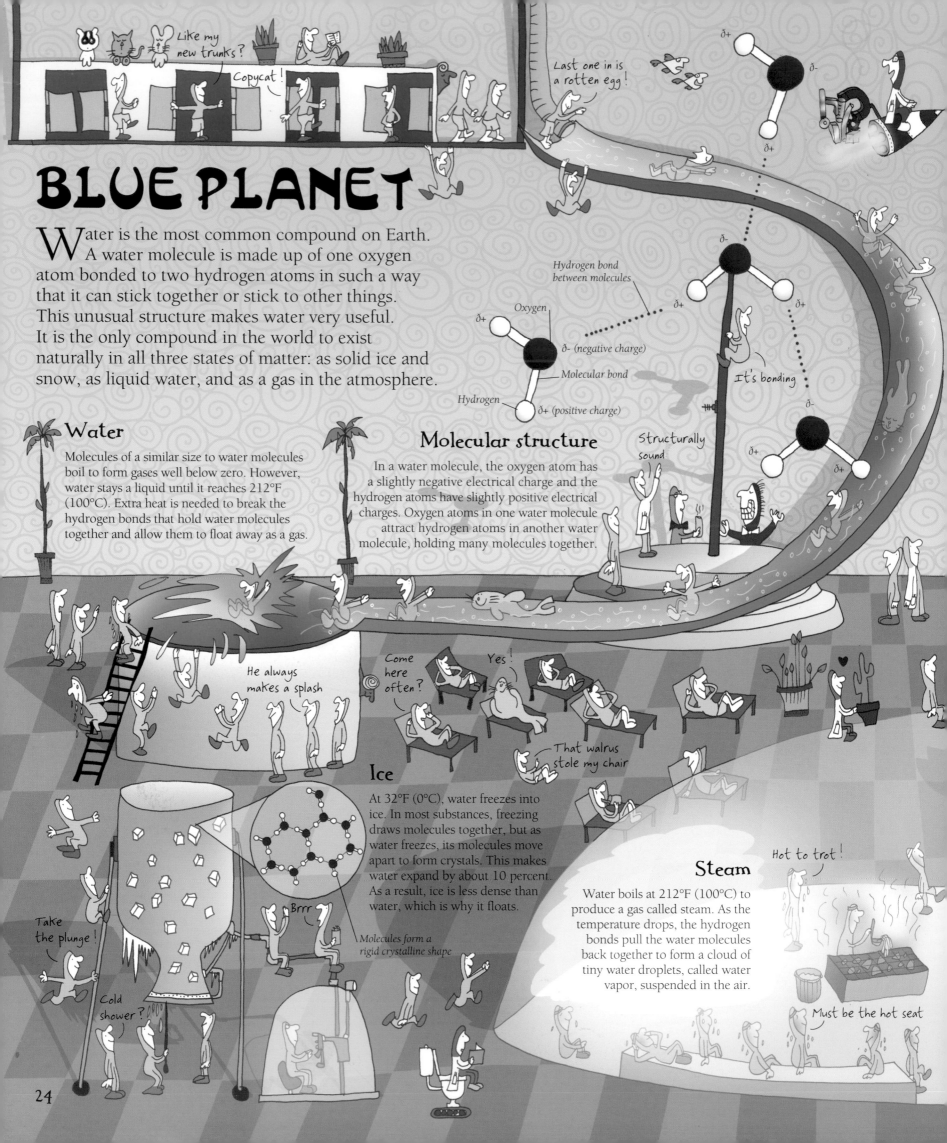

Vital for life

Water is essential to life on Earth. It covers about 70 percent of our planet and exists in every living thing. The world's water supplies are renewed constantly as rain falls, evaporates, becomes cloud, and falls as rain again.

Heating and cooling

The oceans carry heat around the planet, away from the equator and toward the frozen Poles. Lakes and oceans absorb the Sun's heat during the day, and release it at night, so the planet does not experience dramatic temperature swings.

THE BLUE PLANET SPA

Universal solvent

A water molecule's electrical charge attracts molecules of other substances, making them dissolve in water. More substances dissolve in water than in any other solvent. Water is crucial to living things because it transports dissolved nutrients and gases to living cells.

Protective ice

One advantage of ice floating is that it can provide a thick layer of insulation between the external air temperature and the water below. Under the ice, the water is relatively warm, so many creatures can survive.

25

Mixing it up

When two substances are put together without causing a reaction, the result is a mixture. If the blended particles are large, like chunks of fruit in yogurt, it is easy to see the components of the mixture. However, it is difficult to recognize a mixture of tiny particles, such as sugar added to water or gases in the air. A variety of methods can be used to separate the mixture back into its component parts.

Dissolving

A substance has dissolved when it mixes into another substance completely, with every part of the mixture the same. The dissolved matter is called the solute, while the substance it mixed with is called the solvent.

Solute

Solvent

Solvent moving in

Slotting in

The molecules of the solvent move into the space between the molecules of the solute.

Solvent breaks down solute

Breaking apart

The solvent molecules break the bonds of the solute molecules, allowing them to mix together.

Solution

Dissolving

When the solute is evenly mixed with the solvent, the mixture is called a solution.

Good solution

A sprinkle more

Slurp!

That's the last straw

Your round?

No, he's square

Mine's shaken, not stirred

Put your skates on

Cheers!

Do I know you?

I can't watch

ooopps!

Change the record

Saturated solution

There is a limit to the amount of solute that a solvent can dissolve. When all the space between the molecules is used up, no more solute can dissolve. The solution is then called saturated.

Fully booked?

Have a hot toddy

Temperature

Heating a substance makes the molecules move farther apart, creating more space between them. When a solvent is heated, more solute can dissolve before it runs out of room and becomes saturated.

Blue suede shoes

Service with a smile

Coming right up

Suspension

When particles in a mixture are too large to dissolve, they hang suspended in a liquid or gas to form a mixture called a suspension. Smoke is a suspension of burned particles in air.

FIRE!

Groovy

Grrrr

Make it snappy

I've drawn the short straw

Emulsion

Liquids that do not form a solution when mixed together are called immiscible. It is possible to force immiscible liquids to form a suspension, called an emulsion, by shaking them, but they separate into layers eventually.

Colloid

In most suspensions, the suspended particles settle eventually at the bottom, but in a suspension called a colloid, the particles are too small and light to settle. Whipped cream is a colloid of air suspended in liquid.

Separating mixtures

The components of mixtures are not chemically bonded, so it does not take a chemical reaction to separate them. Mixtures are separated using methods that make use of the different physical properties of the components.

DISTILLING CRUDE OIL

68°F (20°C) Gas for fuel

104°F (40°C) Gas for cars

232°F (111°C) Naphtha for chemical production

356°F (180°C) Kerosene for jet fuel

500°F (260°C) Diesel oil for diesel engines

644°F (340°C) Fuel for ships, road surfaces, and paraffin

Heated crude oil

Distillation

Substances with different boiling points can be separated by distillation. The mixture is heated and as it reaches the boiling point of each component, that component evaporates. As it cools, the component turns back into a liquid, ready to be collected.

Chromatography

Chemists sometimes analyze substances in a solution by placing an absorbent solid material inside. The components of the solution travel different distances up the material. Food scientists can use chromatography to discover what colorings have been added to food.

Brilliant blue (blue food dye)

Tartrazine (yellow food dye)

Chromatography paper

Filtration

When a mixture is made of substances with different-sized particles, it can be separated by filtration. The simplest form of filtration is to use a strainer, which allows small particles to fit through the holes, while catching the large ones.

Centrifuging

Substances with varying densities can be separated by centrifuging. The mixture is spun at great speed in a machine, so the denser particles are forced to the bottom of the container, and the lighter particles rise to the top. Blood can be separated in this way.

Lighter liquid plasma

Red blood cells

Centrifuging machine

WARNING! CHEMISTS AT WORK

The test tubes, Bunsen burners, and glass flasks found in a laboratory may not look like anything you have at home, but chemistry is at work in houses all over the world every day—each time you cook, do dishes, wash clothes, or bathe. Your home is also full of materials, such as plastics, fabrics, metals, and glass, that are developed by organic and inorganic chemists.

Chemistry in the home

Around your house are substances that produce chemical reactions when they meet other substances. Some of these substances are so familiar that you do not even think of them as chemicals, for example, soap, self-rising flour, toothpaste, and eggs.

Cleaning

Soap molecules have tails that are attracted to greasy dirt, and heads that are attracted to water. When you wash something, the tails cling to the dirt. The water-loving heads then clean by pulling the dirt apart in the water.

Tails attracted to dirt

This is dirty work

Stop thief!

One won't hurt

I'm as clean as a whistle

Water-loving heads pull the dirt apart

Pooh!

Yum!

Tough cookie

Cooking

Mixing ingredients together before heating them produces chemical reactions that form new substances. A recipe is a little like a chemical equation: you have to measure the ingredients carefully or the recipe will not work—especially in baking.

Medicines

Pharmaceutical chemists use carbon compounds to form medicines, sometimes based on natural substances. From the 5th century BCE, people chewed willow bark as a painkiller. In 1899, chemists discovered salicylic acid, the bark's main ingredient, and used it to create a new artificial painkiller, aspirin.

Carbon

Hydrogen

Oxygen

Salicylic acid molecule

Acetylsalicylic acid molecule (aspirin)

ORGANIC CHEMISTRY

That's added fuel to the fire

Organic chemistry

Carbon, the focus of organic chemistry, is the sixth most common element on Earth. It forms more different compounds than any other element, and carbon compounds are the basis of all living matter.

Carbon

Hydrogen

How fuel-ish

Ethylene molecule

Polythene molecule

Fossil fuels, such as oil, are used in the polymer industry

Meet the new lab technician

I'm as dry as a bone

Fuel

When fuels containing carbon compounds, such as fossil fuels and wood, are burned, they react with oxygen in the air to produce carbon dioxide (CO_2) and heat energy. CO_2 is a pollutant that contributes to global warming, so chemists are trying to find cleaner, greener fuels.

It's oil over the floor!

Polymers

Carbon atoms can combine with hydrogen and other elements to form chain molecules called polymers. Extracted from fossil fuels, polymers such as ethylene are used to form much larger compounds such as polythene, which is used in plastics.

Fossil fuels

Oil   Coal   Gas

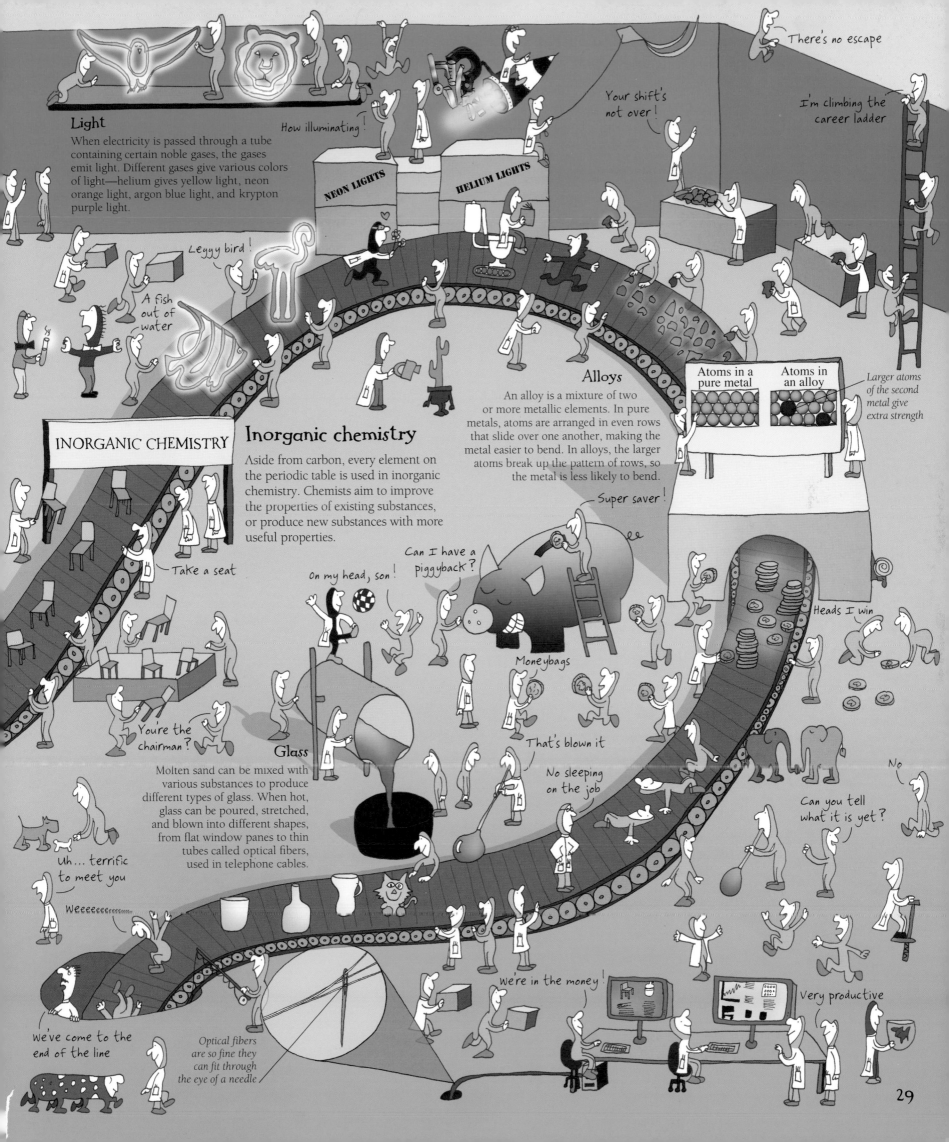

Light

When electricity is passed through a tube containing certain noble gases, the gases emit light. Different gases give various colors of light—helium gives yellow light, neon orange light, argon blue light, and krypton purple light.

Inorganic chemistry

Aside from carbon, every element on the periodic table is used in inorganic chemistry. Chemists aim to improve the properties of existing substances, or produce new substances with more useful properties.

INORGANIC CHEMISTRY

Alloys

An alloy is a mixture of two or more metallic elements. In pure metals, atoms are arranged in even rows that slide over one another, making the metal easier to bend. In alloys, the larger atoms break up the pattern of rows, so the metal is less likely to bend.

Atoms in a pure metal

Atoms in an alloy

Larger atoms of the second metal give extra strength

Glass

Molten sand can be mixed with various substances to produce different types of glass. When hot, glass can be poured, stretched, and blown into different shapes, from flat window panes to thin tubes called optical fibers, used in telephone cables.

Optical fibers are so fine they can fit through the eye of a needle

29

ENDLESS ENERGY

Everything from turning on an electric fan to playing a game uses energy. But for scientists, energy goes beyond making machines work and bodies move. They recognize the energy involved in every process, every chemical reaction, and every living thing. Energy cannot be created or destroyed. Instead, it is just converted into another form of energy.

Forms of energy

Energy comes in many different forms, such as light, heat, sound, electrical, and mechanical energy. All forms of energy can be converted from one form to another.

Potential energy

Stored energy that can be converted into another form of energy in the future is called potential energy. Bouncing down on a trampoline stretches the fabric, giving it potential energy. When the fabric springs back, the trampolinist is flung into the air and the potential energy is released as kinetic energy.

Chemical energy

Molecules are bonded together by a form of potential energy called chemical energy. When these bonds are made and broken by chemical reactions, energy may be released. In the digestive process, chemical energy is released from food for our bodies to use.

Kinetic energy

A moving object, such as a ball, has a form of energy called kinetic energy. The more kinetic energy the object has, the faster it moves. When the object stops moving, it no longer has kinetic energy.

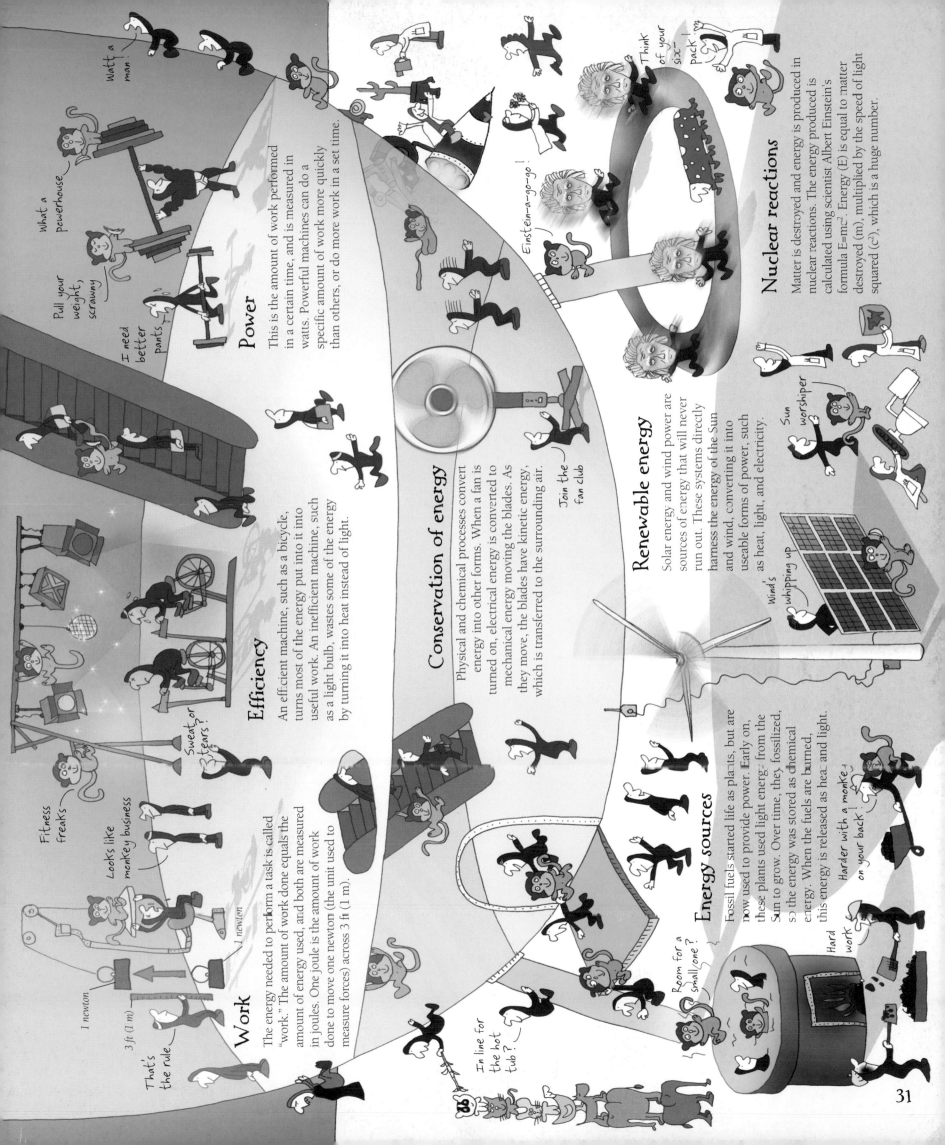

Work

The energy needed to perform a task is called "work." The amount of work done equals the amount of energy used, and both are measured in joules. One joule is the amount of work done to move one newton (the unit used to measure forces) across 3 ft (1 m).

That's the rule

1 newton

1 newton

3 ft (1 m)

Efficiency

An efficient machine, such as a bicycle, turns most of the energy put into it into useful work. An inefficient machine, such as a light bulb, wastes some of the energy by turning it into heat instead of light.

Fitness freaks

Looks like monkey business

Sweat or tears?

Power

This is the amount of work performed in a certain time, and is measured in watts. Powerful machines can do a specific amount of work more quickly than others, or do more work in a set time.

Pull your weight, scrawny

I need better pants

What a powerhouse

Watt a man!

Conservation of energy

Physical and chemical processes convert energy into other forms. When a fan is turned on, electrical energy is converted to mechanical energy moving the blades. As they move, the blades have kinetic energy, which is transferred to the surrounding air.

Join the fan club

In line for the hot tub?

Renewable energy

Solar energy and wind power are sources of energy that will never run out. These systems directly harness the energy of the Sun and wind, converting it into useable forms of power, such as heat, light, and electricity.

Wind's whipping up

Sun worshiper

Energy sources

Fossil fuels started life as plants, but are now used to provide power. Early on, these plants used light energy from the Sun to grow. Over time, they fossilized, so the energy was stored as chemical energy. When the fuels are burned, this energy is released as heat and light.

Room for a small one?

Hard work

Harder with a monkey on your back!

Nuclear reactions

Matter is destroyed and energy is produced in nuclear reactions. The energy produced is calculated using scientist Albert Einstein's formula $E=mc^2$. Energy (E) is equal to matter destroyed (m), multiplied by the speed of light squared (c^2), which is a huge number.

Think of your six-pack!

Einstein-a-go-go!

Good vibrations

The scream of a siren, the rustle of leaves in the wind, the twitter of bird song, and the beat of a drum are just a few of the many sounds you can hear. Sounds are invisible waves of energy that spread out from a source and cause the surrounding air to vibrate. When these waves reach our ears, our brains recognize them as specific sounds.

Measuring waves

Differences in the size and shape of sound waves produce a variety of effects. In a diagram of a sound wave, measurements are taken from a flat horizontal line centered halfway between the peak and trough.

Peak

The highest point that a wave reaches is called the peak.

Trough

The lowest point that a wave reaches is called the trough.

Amplitude

The maximum height of a peak or depth of a trough, measured from the resting position, is called the amplitude.

Wavelength

The distance between two equivalent points on neighboring waves is called the wavelength.

Frequency

The speed at which waves move is called their frequency. This is measured in hertz, with 1 hz being one wave passing a given point each second.

Hearing sounds

When sound waves hit something sensitive to sound, such as an ear or a microphone, they are heard. People detect sounds at 20–20,000 hz, but many animals can detect higher or lower frequencies.

Pitch

The frequency of sound waves affects the pitch of a sound. Deep, low-pitched sounds, such as thunder, are produced by low frequency waves. Shrill, high-pitched sounds, such as a whistle, are produced by high frequency waves.

Volume

When an object or source vibrates with a lot of energy, it produces waves with high amplitude and loud sound. Waves with less energy have low amplitude and sound quieter.

32

Supersonic flight

When a supersonic aircraft reaches the speed of sound, it catches up with its own sound waves. This produces a big bang called a sonic boom, and a halo of water vapor.

Wind instrument

A pure sound and a clean wave form are produced by wind instruments, such as a flute, when blown.

Percussion instrument

Banging a percussion instrument, such as a drum, creates a sharp sound wave and a crashing sound.

Stringed instrument

When the strings on a stringed instrument, such as a harp, are plucked, they vibrate to produce a bright, harmonic sound.

Recording sounds

Sounds are stored by turning sound energy into electrical signals and then recording them. To listen to the sounds, the electrical signals are converted back into sound waves.

Music

Playing a musical instrument produces a pattern of sound waves. Every note has a fundamental pitch, or frequency, but can include many other harmonics—waves at different frequencies that vibrate in harmony with the fundamental pitch.

Doppler effect

Sound waves from an approaching ambulance are high-pitched because they are compressed by the movement. As the ambulance moves off, the waves stretch out and the sound is lower-pitched.

Echoes

When sound waves hit hard surfaces, part of the wave bounces off. The reflected sound travels back and is heard at the source as an echo.

Sound in water

When sound travels through substances denser than air, the closely packed molecules allow the waves to travel faster. Sound travels four times faster in water than in air.

Traveling sound

Sound waves can travel through air, water, or any other type of matter, but they cannot travel where there is no matter—in a vacuum or out in space. The speed of sound in dry air at 32°F (0°C) is 740 mph (1,190 kph).

HEAT WAVE

If you sit by a roaring campfire at night, you can feel the heat sweeping out into the cold air. Thermal (heat) energy is caused by molecules moving inside a substance, and it always spreads out from hotter objects to colder things. For this reason it is a form of kinetic (movement) energy, but it is also potential energy as it can be stored.

Moving molecules

In liquids and gases, molecules can move around freely, so heat makes them flow more quickly, as well as making them vibrate. In a solid, molecules cannot move freely, so heat energy only causes them to vibrate.

Hot

Inside a hot object, the molecules vibrate rapidly. As they move, they knock into molecules around them, transferring heat energy. Something feels hot if its temperature is higher than the temperature of your skin.

Heated molecules vibrating wildly

Cooled molecules moving only slightly

Cold

The colder an object is, the slower its molecules move. Even in a lump of ice, the molecules still possess thermal energy, but they are moving only slightly.

Absolute zero

At a temperature called absolute zero, molecules stop moving. It is not actually possible to cool something this much, because matter cannot exist without movement. However, scientists have managed to create temperatures within a millionth of a degree of absolute zero.

Expansion and contraction

Heated molecules move apart, expanding the substance they are in. Cooling has the opposite effect. Small gaps, called expansion joints, are included in bridges and buildings to provide room for this expanding and contracting.

Thermometer

Changes in temperature outside a thermometer make the liquid inside the glass bulb expand or contract. The level of the liquid in the thermometer is measured by comparing it to a scale on the side.

Mercury rises with the heat

Temp. scale

Glass exterior

Glass bulb

Interior of Sun: 14 million K, 25 million°F, 14 million°C

Surface of Sun: 5,800 K, 9,930°F, 5,500°C

Water boils: 373 K, 212°F, 100°C

Human body temperature: 310 K, 98.6°F, 37°C

Average surface temperature of Earth: 288 K, 59°F, 15°C

Pure water freezes: 273 K, 32°F, 0°C

Freezing point of salt water: 255 K, 0°F, -17.7°C

Lowest temperature recorded on Earth: 184 K, -128°F, -89°C

Absolute zero: 0 K, -459.67°F, -273.15°C

Units of temperature

Three different units are used to measure temperature. Scientists use the Kelvin, which takes absolute zero as 0 K on its scale. Most countries use the Celsius scale, which starts with the freezing point of water as 0°C. The Fahrenheit scale, used in the US, starts at 0°F, the freezing point of saltwater.

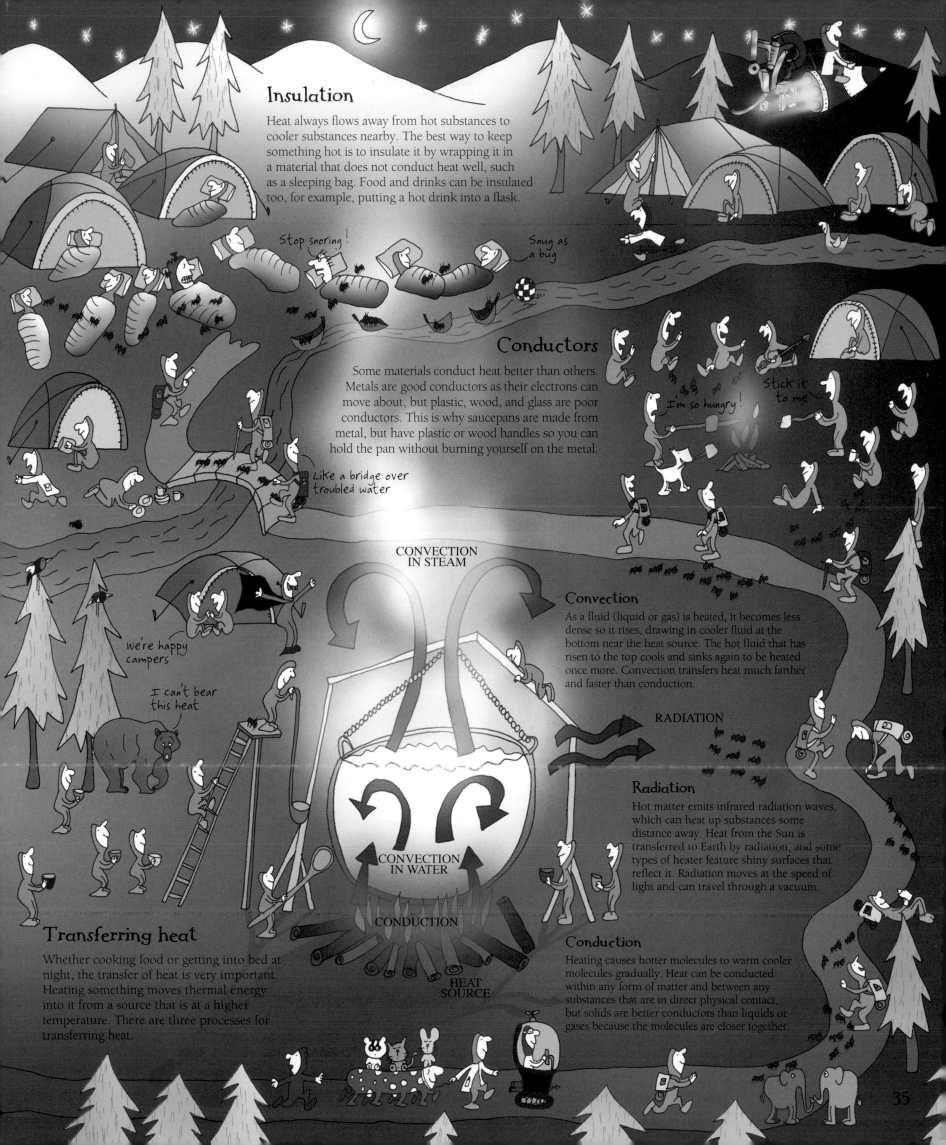

Insulation

Heat always flows away from hot substances to cooler substances nearby. The best way to keep something hot is to insulate it by wrapping it in a material that does not conduct heat well, such as a sleeping bag. Food and drinks can be insulated too, for example, putting a hot drink into a flask.

Conductors

Some materials conduct heat better than others. Metals are good conductors as their electrons can move about, but plastic, wood, and glass are poor conductors. This is why saucepans are made from metal, but have plastic or wood handles so you can hold the pan without burning yourself on the metal.

CONVECTION IN STEAM

Convection

As a fluid (liquid or gas) is heated, it becomes less dense so it rises, drawing in cooler fluid at the bottom near the heat source. The hot fluid that has risen to the top cools and sinks again to be heated once more. Convection transfers heat much farther and faster than conduction.

RADIATION

Radiation

Hot matter emits infrared radiation waves, which can heat up substances some distance away. Heat from the Sun is transferred to Earth by radiation, and some types of heater feature shiny surfaces that reflect it. Radiation moves at the speed of light and can travel through a vacuum.

CONVECTION IN WATER

CONDUCTION

HEAT SOURCE

Transferring heat

Whether cooking food or getting into bed at night, the transfer of heat is very important. Heating something moves thermal energy into it from a source that is at a higher temperature. There are three processes for transferring heat.

Conduction

Heating causes hotter molecules to warm cooler molecules gradually. Heat can be conducted within any form of matter and between any substances that are in direct physical contact, but solids are better conductors than liquids or gases because the molecules are closer together.

35

Telescope

Astronomers use huge reflecting telescopes to look at the night sky. Inside each telescope is a curved mirror, which gathers light from space and reflects it in another mirror into an eyepiece or a camera.

Some light reading

Observed object

Microscope

A mirror at the bottom of a microscope reflects light through the object being observed. This light travels through convex lenses, which magnify the object.

Lenses

Glass or transparent plastic can be shaped into a curved lens, which uses refraction to magnify or reduce objects. Lenses are used in glasses to correct eyesight, and optical instruments, such as telescopes and cameras.

Convex lens

Direction of light rays

Convex lenses

Light is refracted inward by convex lenses, producing an image that may be larger or smaller than the object depending on the distance from the lens. These lenses are used to make refracting telescopes and magnifying glasses.

Concave lens

Direction of light rays

Concave lenses

Light rays are spread out by a concave lens, producing an image that is smaller than the object. These lenses are used in film projectors to make the image spread out and cover a large area of screen.

Refraction

Sluuuurp!

A straw standing in a glass of water appears bent where it enters the water. This is because the speed of light changes as it passes from one transparent material to another, making the light bend slightly.

Bend where the speed of light changes between transparent materials

Irregular reflections

When a reflective surface is not smooth, like a mirrored disco ball, light waves bounce off in all directions, scattering the light and giving no clear image.

They're having a ball!

Let's party!

Care for a dance?

Smaller image is produced

Convex mirror

Object

on reflection...

Convex mirrors

A mirror that curves out in the center, like the surface of a ball, is called a convex mirror. This type of mirror produces an image that is smaller than the object.

Enlarged image is reflected

Object is close up

Concave mirror

Upside-down image is reflected

Object is far away

Concave mirror

Concave mirrors

A mirror that curves like the inside of a bowl is called a concave mirror. When an object is far away from a concave mirror, its image appears upside down and smaller. As the object gets closer, its image gets bigger.

Light ray

Object

Reflected ray

Reflected image

Mirror

Mirrors

Almost all the light that falls on a mirror is reflected back. The reflected light rays form a reversed image, which appears to be the same distance behind the mirror as the reflected object is in front.

Reflection

A time to reflect

If you look at a smooth, shiny surface, you can see reflections of the objects around it. These reflections happen because most of the light that hits a shiny surface bounces back off.

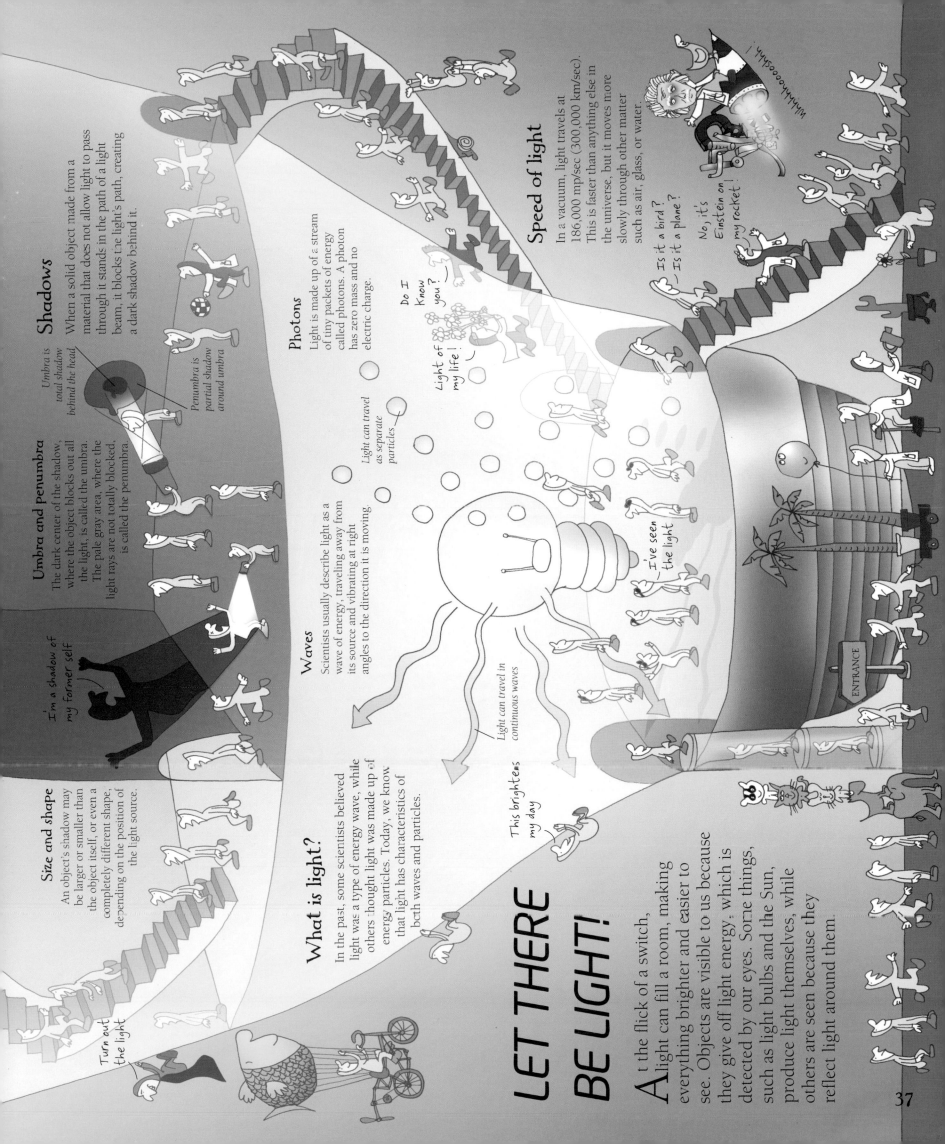

LET THERE BE LIGHT!

At the flick of a switch, a light can fill a room, making everything brighter and easier to see. Objects are visible to us because they give off light energy, which is detected by our eyes. Some things, such as light bulbs and the Sun, produce light themselves, while others are seen because they reflect light around them.

What is light?

In the past, some scientists believed light was a type of energy wave, while others thought light was made up of energy particles. Today, we know that light has characteristics of both waves and particles.

Waves

Scientists usually describe light as a wave of energy, traveling away from its source and vibrating at right angles to the direction it is moving.

Light can travel in continuous waves

Photons

Light is made up of a stream of tiny packets of energy called photons. A photon has zero mass and no electric charge.

Light can travel as separate particles

Shadows

When a solid object made from a material that does not allow light to pass through it stands in the path of a light beam, it blocks the light's path, creating a dark shadow behind it.

Umbra and penumbra

The dark center of the shadow, where the object blocks out all the light, is called the umbra. The pale gray area, where the light rays are not totally blocked, is called the penumbra.

Umbra is total shadow behind the head

Penumbra is partial shadow around umbra

Size and shape

An object's shadow may be larger or smaller than the object itself, or even a completely different shape, depending on the position of the light source.

I'm a shadow of my former self

Turn out the light

Speed of light

In a vacuum, light travels at 186,000 mp/sec (300,000 km/sec). This is faster than anything else in the universe, but it moves more slowly through other matter such as air, glass, or water.

Is it a bird? Is it a plane?

No, it's Einstein on my rocket!

whhhhooooshhh...

Do I know you?

Light of my life!

I've seen the light

This brightens my day

ENTRANCE

37

Beyond the rainbow

The waves of energy you see as light are only a small part of a larger range of energy waves called electromagnetic radiation. Just as our ears can only hear certain wavelengths of sound, our eyes can detect the wavelength of visible light, but cannot detect longer electromagnetic wavelengths such as radio waves or shorter wavelengths such as X-rays.

Electromagnetic spectrum

All electromagnetic waves travel at the speed of light, and are made from photons (energy particles). The difference between them is their wavelengths, frequencies, and energy levels. The electromagnetic spectrum arranges the waves in order of wavelength.

Microwaves   Infrared radiation   Visible spectrum   Ultraviolet radiation

ELECTROMAGNETIC SPECTRUM

Radio waves

Gamma rays

X-rays

It's electro-magical!

Radio waves

The waves with the longest wavelength, lowest frequency, and lowest energy are radio waves. These carry radio, television, and cell phone signals around the world. Longest of all are the radio waves that come from outer space, which are picked up by radio telescopes on Earth.

Infrared radiation

The word "infrared" means "beyond the red," because these waves are found just past red light in the electromagnetic spectrum. This energy radiates from warm objects, which we detect as heat. Infrared detectors are used in medicine to provide a thermal (heat) body map, and night-vision devices detect infrared coming from warm bodies and vehicles.

INFRARED TUNNEL

Microwaves

Blasting microwave energy through food makes the water molecules inside vibrate more quickly, heating it up. Microwaves are also used to transmit phone and television signals via telecommunications satellites, and in radar systems for locating ships, aircraft, and tracking weather systems.

Visible spectrum

The part of the electromagnetic spectrum that human eyes can detect is called the visible spectrum. Earth's atmosphere reflects most electromagnetic wavelengths from space away, but all the wavelengths of the visible spectrum can pass through, bringing us light from the Sun and stars.

What a ride!

Turn that noise off!

I can't look

I shouldn't have eaten that hot dog

Arrrgghh!

Give me a wave

Ready

Tastes like chicken

Everything does

I should floss my teeth after this

Bluuhhh!

Colorama

Colors

An object appears to be a particular color because it absorbs some wavelengths of light and reflects the other wavelengths. We only see the wavelengths that are reflected. Pink and brown, which cannot be seen as part of the visible spectrum, are made up of a mixture of different wavelengths.

A white object reflects all wavelengths of light and absorbs no light.

A yellow object absorbs every color except yellow, which it reflects.

A black object absorbs all wavelengths of light and reflects no light.

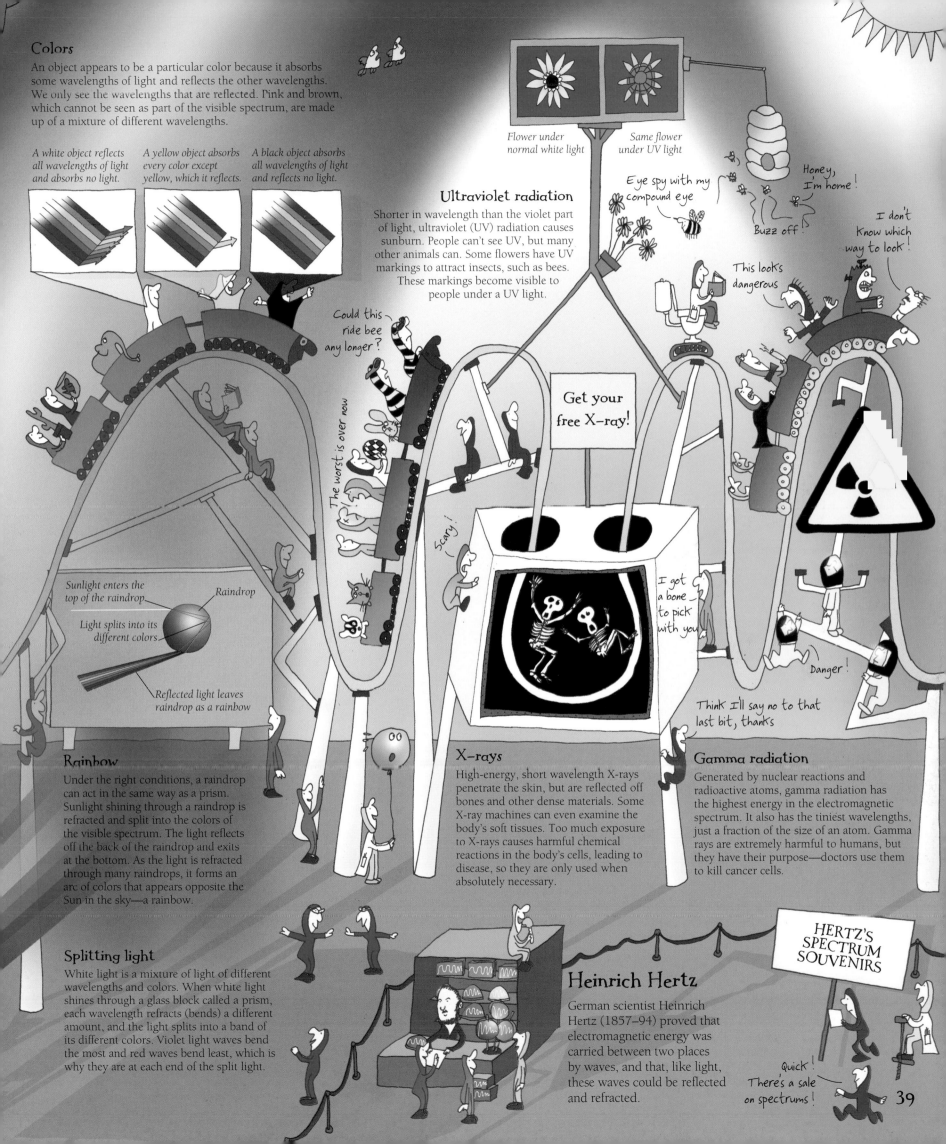

Flower under normal white light

Same flower under UV light

Ultraviolet radiation

Shorter in wavelength than the violet part of light, ultraviolet (UV) radiation causes sunburn. People can't see UV, but many other animals can. Some flowers have UV markings to attract insects, such as bees. These markings become visible to people under a UV light.

Get your free X-ray!

Sunlight enters the top of the raindrop

Raindrop

Light splits into its different colors

Reflected light leaves raindrop as a rainbow

Rainbow

Under the right conditions, a raindrop can act in the same way as a prism. Sunlight shining through a raindrop is refracted and split into the colors of the visible spectrum. The light reflects off the back of the raindrop and exits at the bottom. As the light is refracted through many raindrops, it forms an arc of colors that appears opposite the Sun in the sky—a rainbow.

X-rays

High-energy, short wavelength X-rays penetrate the skin, but are reflected off bones and other dense materials. Some X-ray machines can even examine the body's soft tissues. Too much exposure to X-rays causes harmful chemical reactions in the body's cells, leading to disease, so they are only used when absolutely necessary.

Gamma radiation

Generated by nuclear reactions and radioactive atoms, gamma radiation has the highest energy in the electromagnetic spectrum. It also has the tiniest wavelengths, just a fraction of the size of an atom. Gamma rays are extremely harmful to humans, but they have their purpose—doctors use them to kill cancer cells.

Splitting light

White light is a mixture of light of different wavelengths and colors. When white light shines through a glass block called a prism, each wavelength refracts (bends) a different amount, and the light splits into a band of its different colors. Violet light waves bend the most and red waves bend least, which is why they are at each end of the split light.

HERTZ'S SPECTRUM SOUVENIRS

Heinrich Hertz

German scientist Heinrich Hertz (1857–94) proved that electromagnetic energy was carried between two places by waves, and that, like light, these waves could be reflected and refracted.

Brute force

Whether throwing a snowball or skating on ice, every action requires a force to create the movement. A force is a push or pull that causes an object to change its speed or direction. Forces control every movement in the universe, from huge planets right down to tiny atoms. Some forces act directly on an object, such as pulling a sled, while others act at a distance, such as the force of gravity keeping the stars in motion.

Isaac Newton

The unit used for measuring forces is the newton (n), named after English scientist Isaac Newton (1642–1727), who came up with the three laws of motion.

Movement

If you start pushing a ball of snow along, it will begin to roll and get bigger. Your push creates a force that acts on the snowball, causing it to move.

Direction

A force can change the direction of a movement. If an object moving in a straight line hits an obstacle, the force created by the impact sends the object bouncing off in a different direction.

Balanced forces

When an object is still, all the forces acting on it are balanced. If you stand on a flat surface, the force of gravity pulling you down is equal to the force of the ground pushing you up, so you stay still.

Full force

A group of people all pulling together can move a much heavier sled than one person can. This is because the bigger the force that acts on something is, the more movement it will create.

Three laws of motion

Isaac Newton's laws explain how forces affect the direction or speed of objects. Scientists call any change of direction or speed an "acceleration," even when the object gets slower.

First law

Newton's first law states that a still object will remain still until a force acts upon it, and an object moving along at a steady speed in a straight line will continue moving at the same speed and in the same direction until a force acts upon it.

Inertia

The tendency of objects to resist changes in motion is called inertia. The heavier an object, the more inertia it has, so it is harder to move heavy objects than light ones.

He's a well-balanced young Brainwave

You gotta roll with it...

OUCH!

Light as a feather

Let's switch

This relationship is going downhill

Yodelay–hee–hoo!

Wow

Dreadful display

You sound a little husky

Easy does it

→ MOVEMENT

Get your skates on

Such chiseled features

ISAAC NEWTON

Chip off the old block

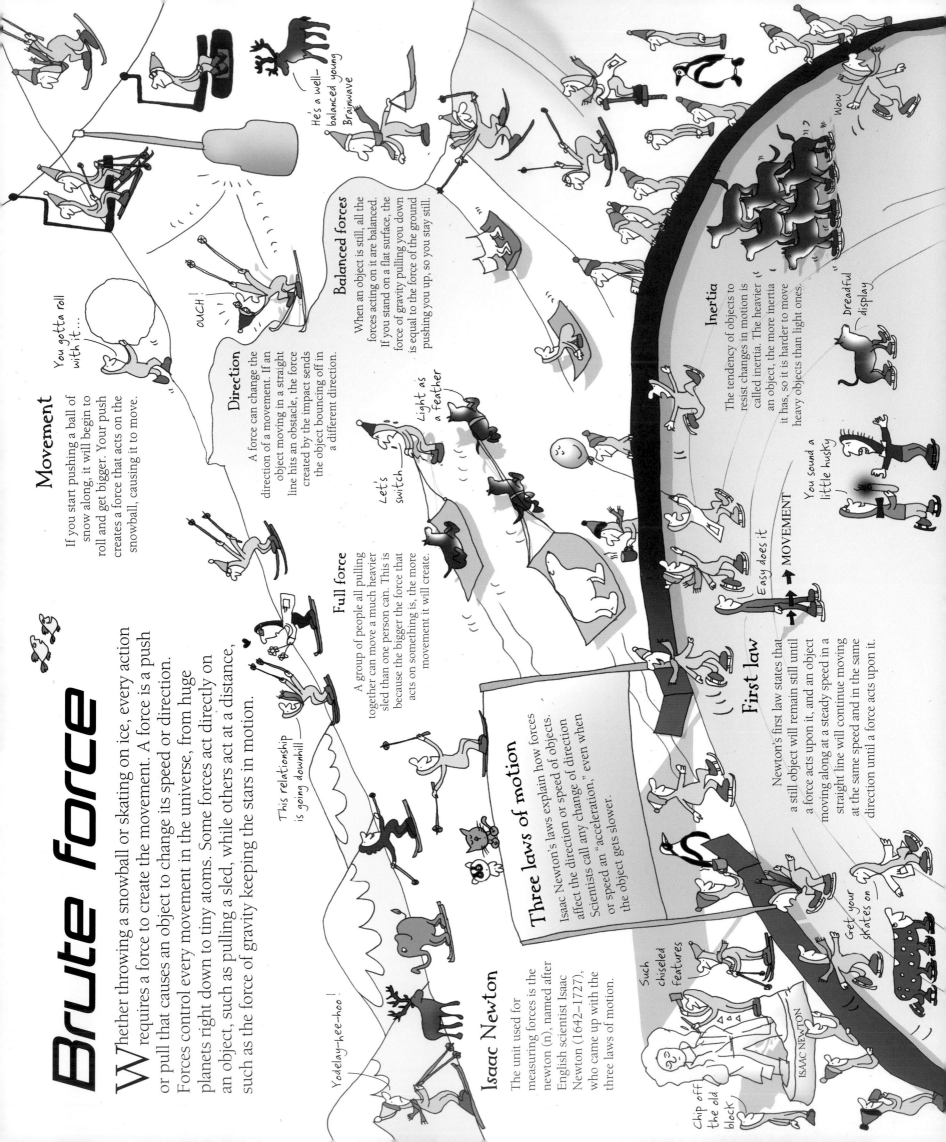

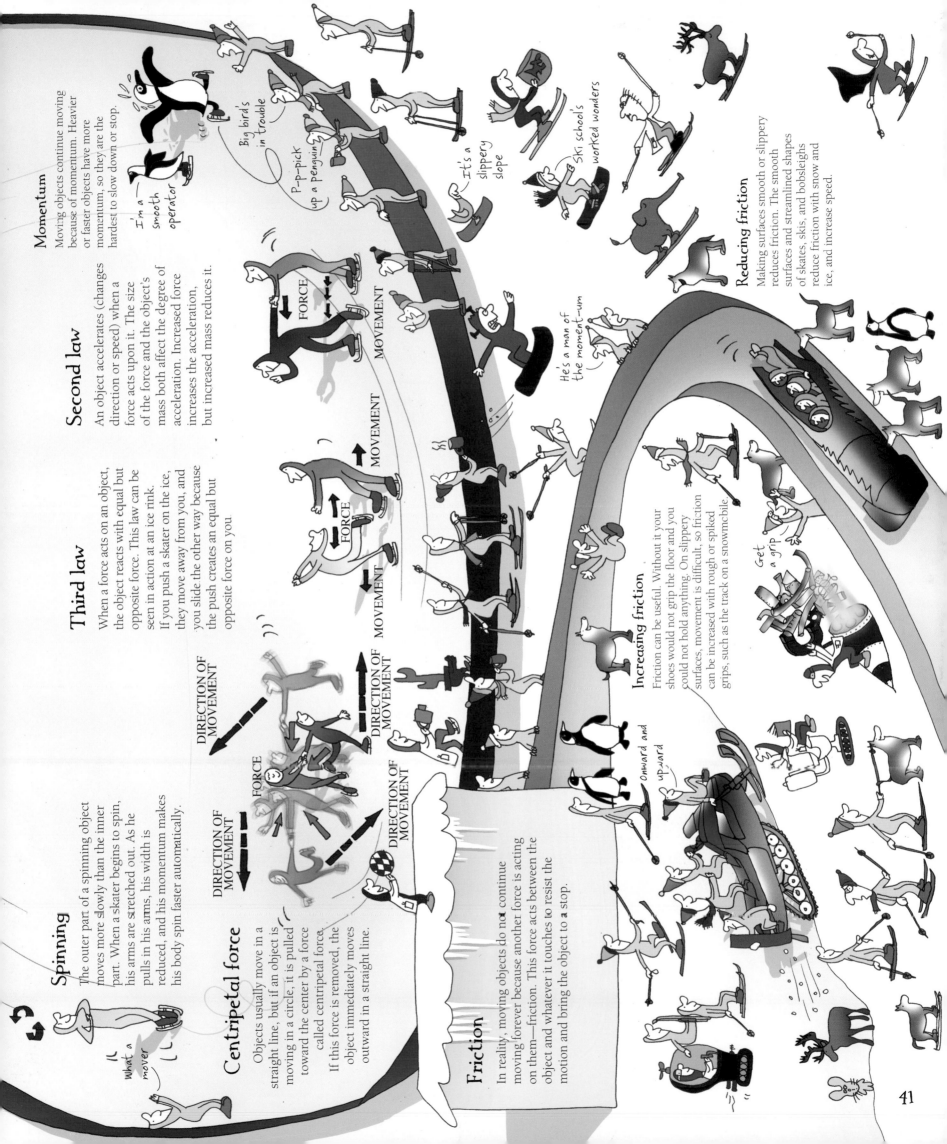

Momentum

Moving objects continue moving because of momentum. Heavier or faster objects have more momentum, so they are the hardest to slow down or stop.

Second law

An object accelerates (changes direction or speed) when a force acts upon it. The size of the force and the object's mass both affect the degree of acceleration. Increased force increases the acceleration, but increased mass reduces it.

Third law

When a force acts on an object, the object reacts with equal but opposite force. This law can be seen in action at an ice rink. If you push a skater on the ice, they move away from you, and you slide the other way because the push creates an equal but opposite force on you

Spinning

The outer part of a spinning object moves more slowly than the inner part. When a skater begins to spin, his arms are stretched out. As he pulls in his arms, his width is reduced, and his momentum makes his body spin faster automatically.

Centripetal force

Objects usually move in a straight line, but if an object is moving in a circle, it is pulled toward the center by a force called centripetal force. If this force is removed, the object immediately moves outward in a straight line.

Friction

In reality, moving objects do not continue moving forever because another force is acting on them—friction. This force acts between the object and whatever it touches to resist the motion and bring the object to a stop.

Increasing friction

Friction can be useful. Without it your shoes would not grip the floor and you could not hold anything. On slippery surfaces, movement is difficult, so friction can be increased with rough or spiked grips, such as the track on a snowmobile.

Reducing friction

Making surfaces smooth or slippery reduces friction. The smooth surfaces and streamlined shapes of skates, skis, and bobsleighs reduce friction with snow and ice, and increase speed.

It's a slippery slope

Ski school's worked wonders

I'm a smooth operator

Big birds in trouble

P-p-pick up a penguin

He's a man of the moment-um

Get a grip

Onward and upward

What a mover

FORCE

MOVEMENT

DIRECTION OF MOVEMENT

41

HARD AT WORK

To lift a heavy weight, like a full suitcase, is really hard work, so many big suitcases have wheels to make them easier to move. The weight of the suitcase has not changed, but it takes less force to move it using the wheels, so you don't need to work so hard. Scientists use the word "machine" to describe any device that makes work easier by changing the forces applied to it.

Simple machines

Each simple machine allows us to push or pull things over increased distances. These machines may alter the direction of a force, like a crowbar converting a pushing force into a pulling force, or a corkscrew changing a turn into a pull. Other machines alter a force's size: the force of a big hammer blow is transformed into the smaller forward movement of a nail when hit.

Pulleys

Cranes can lift heavy weights by using a machine called a pulley. The load is attached to a rope or metal cable looped around a wheel. When a force is applied to the rope, it lifts the load.

Simple pulley

With just one wheel, a simple pulley does not reduce the effort needed to raise a load, but changes the direction of the force.

Load

The load is the object that is moved or balanced by the machine. In most machines, the load moves farther than the force required to move it.

Work done

You can figure out how much work has been done by multiplying the distance an object is moved by the force needed to move it. The same amount of energy can be used to move a large load a small distance, or a small load a long distance.

Ramp

Since ancient times, ramps (also called inclined planes) have been used to raise heavy loads. A load moves a longer distance up a ramp than it would if it were lifted by a person, but the force needed to move it up the ramp is smaller than the force needed to lift it up vertically.

Screw

You have to turn a screw many times to move it forward just a little bit. However, the force of the forward movement is much greater than the force you apply to turn it.

Complex machines

The mechanical devices we normally think of as machines—such as cars, bicycles, cranes, and diggers—contain several simple machines acting together. Scientists call these devices complex (or compound) machines.

Wheel and axle

If an effort is applied to the axle (center) of a wheel, the outer rim of the wheel turns farther and faster than the axle. If the force is applied to the outer rim of the wheel, the axle turns with more force but not so far or fast.

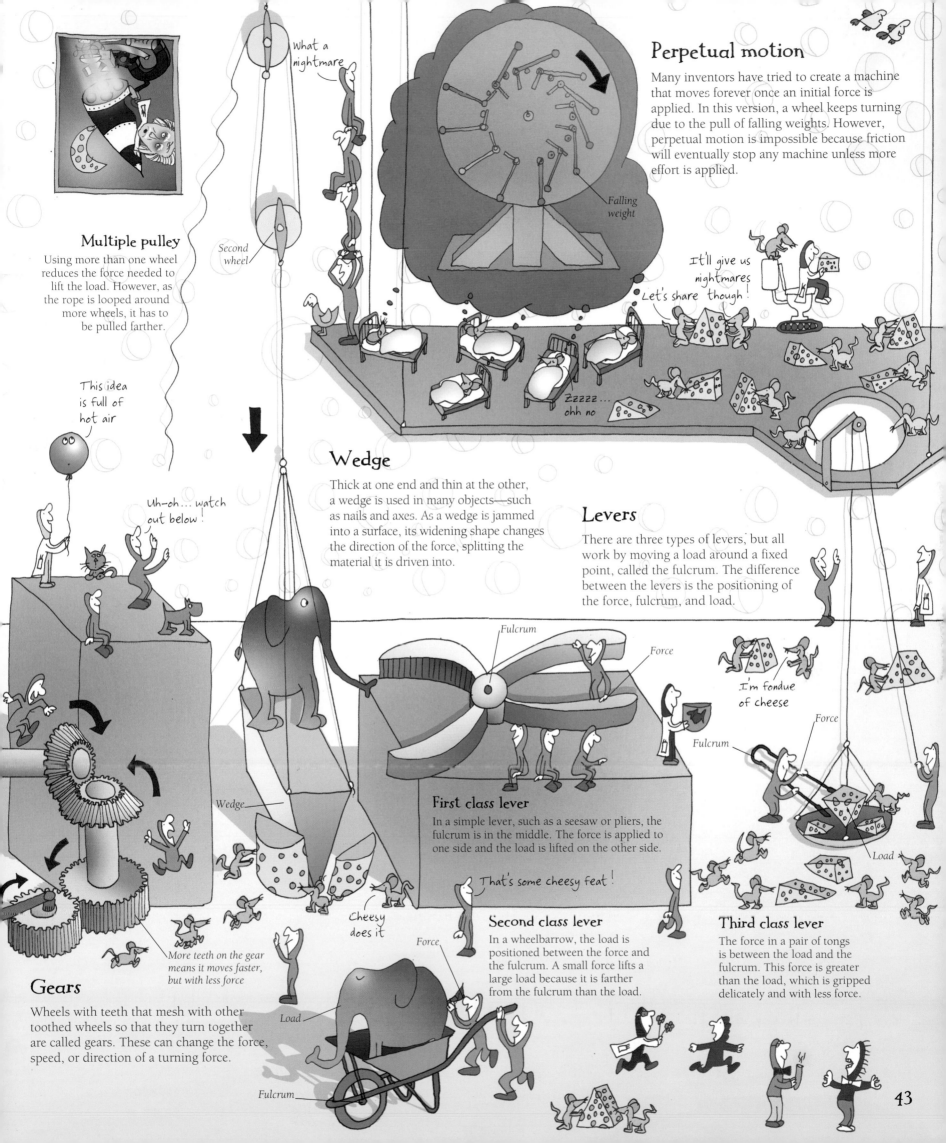

Multiple pulley

Using more than one wheel reduces the force needed to lift the load. However, as the rope is looped around more wheels, it has to be pulled farther.

Perpetual motion

Many inventors have tried to create a machine that moves forever once an initial force is applied. In this version, a wheel keeps turning due to the pull of falling weights. However, perpetual motion is impossible because friction will eventually stop any machine unless more effort is applied.

Wedge

Thick at one end and thin at the other, a wedge is used in many objects—such as nails and axes. As a wedge is jammed into a surface, its widening shape changes the direction of the force, splitting the material it is driven into.

Levers

There are three types of levers, but all work by moving a load around a fixed point, called the fulcrum. The difference between the levers is the positioning of the force, fulcrum, and load.

First class lever

In a simple lever, such as a seesaw or pliers, the fulcrum is in the middle. The force is applied to one side and the load is lifted on the other side.

Second class lever

In a wheelbarrow, the load is positioned between the force and the fulcrum. A small force lifts a large load because it is farther from the fulcrum than the load.

Third class lever

The force in a pair of tongs is between the load and the fulcrum. This force is greater than the load, which is gripped delicately and with less force.

Gears

Wheels with teeth that mesh with other toothed wheels so that they turn together are called gears. These can change the force, speed, or direction of a turning force.

43

Zero gravity

Astronauts orbiting Earth float around their spacecraft, apparently weightless. This state is known as "zero gravity," but, in fact, Earth's gravity is still acting on them. The astronauts are falling continuously toward Earth, but as their spacecraft travels forward, the amount they fall is equal to the amount Earth's surface curves away below them, so they remain floating at the same height above the planet.

Planetary orbits

The immense gravity of the Sun pulls on the planets around it. The planets have enough mass to prevent them from falling into the Sun, but not enough to break away from it, so they are trapped in orbit around the Sun.

Moonwalker

Birdbrain

Falling

If you drop a ball and a feather on Earth, the heavier ball lands first. But in space, where there is no air to slow the feather down, gravity makes everything fall at the same speed, so they land together.

I need some Space

Help yourself!

BLAAAST OFFFFF!

Tides

The Moon's gravity pulls on Earth's oceans, while the planet's spin creates a bulge in the waters on the other side. These bulges move around Earth as it turns, creating the rise and fall of the tides twice a day.

Tide
Earth
Tide
Pull of the Moon
Moon

The tides are turning

It's the final countdown

Prepared for launch?

Ready as I'll ever be

IT'S ALL RELATIVE

I f you jump up in the air, you'll soon fall back down. This is because of gravity—a force so strong it even keeps planets moving in space. From these spinning planets to the tiniest atoms, everything is constantly moving. As a result, any motion is always relative (comparable) to something else.

Must have been that chocolate cake

Mass and weight

Weight is a downward force caused by an object's mass and gravity acting on it. An astronaut has the same mass on the Moon and on Earth, but he weighs less on the Moon, because gravity is weaker there.

NO FOOD

Gravity

The force of gravity acts between bodies, pulling them toward each other. The greater the mass of an object, the more matter it contains, and the stronger its force of gravity. Therefore, objects with greater mass pull harder than objects with less mass. Things fall when you let go of them because the vast mass of planet Earth pulls everything toward it.

Birth of stars

A star forms in a cloud of gas and dust called a nebula. Gravity pulls matter into clumps and compresses it until it is hot and dense enough to trigger nuclear reactions. The reactions produce heat and light, turning a clump of matter into a shining star.

Black holes

A dying star may collapse to form a region of powerful gravity called a black hole. As black holes even suck in light, they can only be seen by observing the effect of their gravity on nearby objects. Anything approaching a black hole is stretched thin as gravity sucks it in.

Albert Einstein

German-born scientist Albert Einstein (1879–1955) came up with ideas about gravity, motion, space, and time that were so extraordinary and different from other people's ideas that some scientists did not accept them at first.

Space and time shown as a stretchy sheet of rubber

Planet Earth, being a heavy object, leaves a dip in space and time

The Moon follows curve of space and gets trapped in orbit around Earth, unable to get out of the dip

Relativity

One of Einstein's ideas is called "relativity" because everything is moving all the time, so motion is always relative to something else. For example, if Spacecraft 1 passes a planet at 10,000 mph (16,090 kph), and Spacecraft 2 passes the same planet at 20,000 mph (32,190 kph), Spacecraft 2 is only going at 10,000 mph (16,090 kph) relative to Spacecraft 1.

Bending space

Einstein explained gravity in a new way. He said that a mass bends the space and time around it, like a ball sitting on a stretchy rubber sheet. Larger masses cause larger distortions, making smaller objects and even light fall toward them with the force we call gravity.

Near the speed of light

It is impossible for anything other than light itself to travel at the speed of light. However, according to Einstein, as an object approaches the speed of light, it shrinks in length but increases in mass, and time slows down.

Time travel

If a spaceship traveled away from Earth for a year at 99.99 percent of the speed of light, time would slow down so much that when the ship and passengers returned home, 72 years would have passed for people on Earth.

POWERFUL ATTRACTION

Push a paperclip toward a magnet with one finger. When it is close, but not quite touching, the paperclip moves toward the magnet and sticks to it. If you try pulling the paperclip off, you feel the magnet's force resisting. This incredible force of attraction is vital to everyday devices such as computers and headphones, but it also helps travelers find their way, and even affects the way the Earth and its atmosphere interact.

Magnetic materials

A substance that can be attracted by a magnet is called a magnetic material. Some of these materials are magnets themselves. Others become magnets when they are near to or touching a magnet, but then lose their magnetism when they move away.

Lodestone

More than 2,500 years ago, the ancient Greeks discovered a naturally occurring magnetic rock called lodestone (or magnetite) that could attract metals and be attracted itself.

Iron

Alloys (mixtures) of iron make good permanent magnets, but pure iron can only be a temporary magnet, because, although easily magnetized when placed near other magnets, it quickly loses its magnetism.

Steel

Many permanent magnets are made from steel—an alloy of iron, carbon, and other metals. Steel is much harder than iron and retains its magnetism for a long time.

That's clip art

Neodymium

Powerful neodymium magnets inside headphones help to produce sound. A neodymium magnet the size of a coin can lift a 22-lb (10-kg) weight.

Stunning!

Magnetic field

The area around a magnet that is affected by the force is called the magnetic field. Iron filings around a magnet form a pattern showing how the direction and strength of the force varies within the field.

I feel drawn to this room

Magnetic field around magnet

OPPOSITE POLES ATTRACT

North end

South end

Attractive!

SAME POLES REPEL

I'm repelled

Poles

The magnetic field is strongest at the two ends of the magnet, called the north and south poles. The north pole is the end that would point north if the magnet were allowed to swing freely.

Attraction

When two magnets are brought together, their opposite poles—a north and a south—are attracted to each other. Iron filings show how the two magnetic fields interact, joining one magnet's north pole to the other magnet's south pole.

Repulsion

When two poles of the same kind—north and north or south and south—are brought together, they push apart, or repel each other. Scattered iron filings show a gap between the magnetic fields, where each field repels the other.

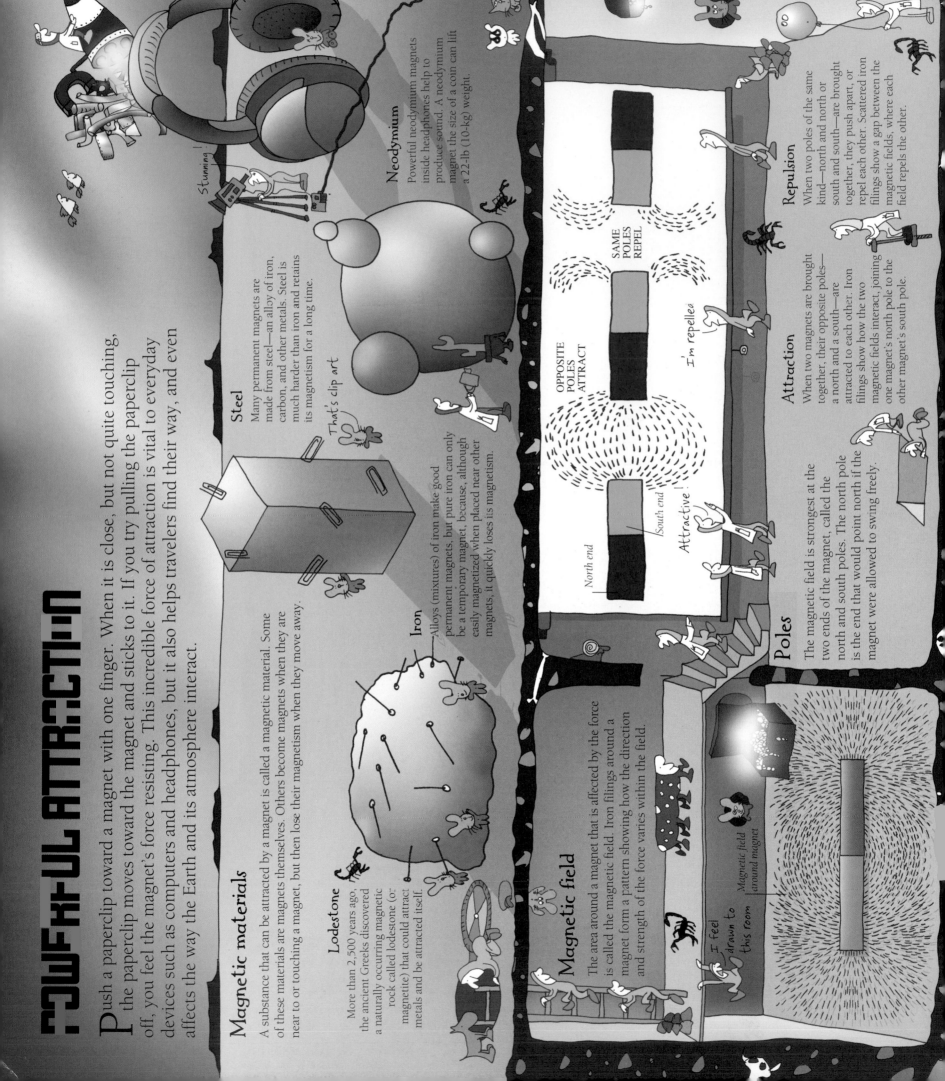

Earth's magnetic field

Planet Earth behaves like a huge magnet, surrounded by a magnetic field called the magnetosphere, which extends out into space. The field is probably created by charged material circulating deep inside the planet.

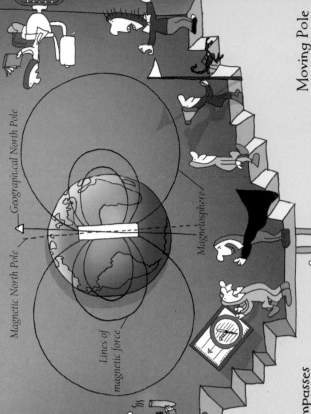

Geographical North Pole
Magnetic North Pole
Magnetosphere
Lines of magnetic force

Moving Pole

The Magnetic North Pole is not in the same place as the geographical North Pole, but in northern Canada. The precise location is unknown, because Earth's magnetic field moves over time and is now traveling at up to 25 miles (40 km) per year.

Compasses

The fine magnetic needle inside a compass spins on a pivot and always points toward Earth's Magnetic North Pole. Chinese and European sailors first used compasses made from lodestone in the 12th century.

Auroras

Patterns of swirling lights sometimes fill the sky near the magnetic poles. These effects, called the Aurora Borealis (Northern Lights) and Aurora Australis (Southern Lights), happen when high-energy photons from the Sun are attracted to the poles, making atoms in the atmosphere glow.

Ooooh!   Aaahh!

Magnetic domains

Inside magnetic materials are regions called magnetic domains. These resemble tiny magnets each with a north and south pole. When the material is unmagnetized, the poles of the domains point randomly in any direction, so the material has no overall north and south pole.

Magnetic domains

UNMAGNETIZED

MAGNETIZED

Magnetizing

When a magnetic material is placed in a magnetic field, the magnetic domains line up so that all the north poles point in one direction and all the south poles in the opposite direction, turning it into a magnet.

Domains aligned by stroking with another magnet

Lining up domains

A magnetic material can become a magnet by stroking it repeatedly in one direction with one pole of a magnet. This lines up the magnetic domains within the material.

Demagnetizing

Striking a magnet hard mixes up the magnetic domains, demagnetizing the magnet. When heated, magnets also become demagnetized because moving molecules in the hot material destroy the alignment of the domains.

Mixed-up domains

Keep out!

Keeper

A horseshoe magnet is bent so that its north and south poles face the same direction. Putting an iron plate called a keeper across the poles forms a magnetic circuit, which keeps the domains aligned and prevents the magnet from gradually losing its magnetism.

Horseshoe magnet

Iron keeper becomes magnetized

Look out!

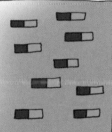

Lightning

Particles of ice swirling around inside storm clouds build up static electricity. Electrons collect at the bottom of the cloud, creating a huge negative charge, which discharges by leaping to something on the ground, such as a metal rod or a tree.

Sparks and shocks

If you walk across a nylon carpet with plastic-soled shoes, your body builds up a static charge as the plastic and carpet rub together. When you touch something metal, the static electricity suddenly discharges (flows away) from your body, giving you a tingling shock, and may even produce a spark.

Clingy clothes

Some clothes build up static by rubbing against your body as you move. These electric charges make the fabric cling uncomfortably to your body, or stick to itself. Fine fabrics such as silk, viscose, and nylon are most likely to have this effect.

Sticky static

Static electricity can be built up by rubbing a balloon against fur, wool, or hair. The balloon becomes negatively charged as it gains electrons, and the material being rubbed becomes positively charged because it loses them. As opposite charges attract, the two stick to each other.

Static electricity

Electrons sometimes fall off one object and stick to another one nearby. This changes the balance of electrons in some of the atoms of both objects, which results in the buildup of an electric charge. This buildup of charge is called static electricity.

Lightning conductor

A metal rod, called a lightning conductor, is fixed on the highest point of tall structures to protect them from lightning. If lightning strikes the rod, the charge drains harmlessly away down a wire to the ground.

SHOCKING BEHAVIOR

Electricity does not just magically appear—it's all around you, inside every atom, all of the time. Electrons do many shocking things when they are broken off from their atoms, and can be harnessed to power almost everything that we use.

The nucleus contains six positively charged protons (green), and six neutrons (red) that do not carry a charge

Six electrons orbit the nucleus, with each one carrying a negative charge

ATOM

Charged particles

Under normal conditions, atoms have no overall electric charge because the number of negatively charged electrons is balanced by the number of positively charged protons.

48

Current electricity

Electrons can move freely between the atoms of metals and some other materials, forming a flow of electricity called a current. This continuous flow of electricity is used to power electrical devices.

I'm a ghost-writer!

Turning the switch on makes the electrons move in the same direction, which makes the light go on

You have the power

Off
On

Down boy

When the free electrons move randomly, the current does not flow

When the free electrons all move in one direction, the current flows

Electrical insulators

Materials called insulators allow little or no electricity to pass through them. Plastic, glass, and ceramics are good insulators, and are used to coat electric components to stop current from flowing out of them.

Ceramic insulators prevent current from flowing away from metal cables on electricity pylons

Plastic insulator

Electrical conductors

Materials or objects that carry current are called conductors. Metals are the best conductors, because electrons move freely between their atoms. Most electric cables are made from copper wire, surrounded by a plastic insulator.

Don't be such a chicken

Conducting wire is wound tightly inside

We've created a monster

Crocodile clip used to transfer electricity

Daddy!

Stop being so creepy

Can we call him "Frank"?

It's alive!

Superconductor

Some materials lose all resistance and allow current to flow freely when they are cooled to very cold temperatures—usually less than -436°F (-260°C). These materials, called superconductors, are used in the huge magnets found in medical scanners.

Resistance

The measure of how easily materials allow current to flow is called resistance. Electrons moving through resistant material lose energy and slow down. Insulators are very resistant, while conductors have little resistance.

Wooohhhooooo

Let's throw some light on the situation

Too scary, I'm gone

Bat's all, folks

It's chilling

MRI (magnetic resonance imaging) scans are produced using superconductors in scanners

Wood is an insulator, allowing little or no current to pass

A good conductor such as metal wire allows current to pass easily

BRIGHT SPARKS

Was there life before the light bulb? The first homes were electrified in the 1880s, but up until then, heat came from dirty coal and wood, light from smelly gas, and all the housework was done by hand. As you watch television, blow-dry your hair, or stuff your clothes in the washing machine, thank your lucky stars for clean, efficient electricity!

Battery

Wire

Switch turns the current off by breaking the circuit

Bulb

Current affairs

Electric circuit

An electric current can only flow if it has a complete pathway called a circuit to move around. A circuit must include a power source, such as a battery, to drive the current, and a conductor for the current to flow through. If there are any gaps in the circuit or the power runs out, the current stops flowing.

Series circuit

This circuit is a continuous loop. The bulbs reduce the amount of current flowing through the circuit, making each bulb shine dimly. If one bulb fails, the circuit is broken and both bulbs go out.

Battery

Wire

Bulb   *Bulb*

Parallel circuit

Here, the current flows around two separate paths. With only one bulb in each path, there is less resistance, so each bulb is brighter. If one bulb fails, current still flows through the other, so it will stay lit.

Battery

Wire   *Bulb*

Bulb

Using electricity

Most household devices that use energy are powered by electricity. This is because electricity can easily be converted into different forms of energy, such as heat, sound, light, or kinetic (movement) energy.

What a tangled web

Heat

Inside an iron, a current passes through a heating element (similar to the one in an electric kettle) made from a material with a high resistance. As the element resists the current's flow, the electrical energy is converted to heat, and the iron warms up.

What a sizzler

Look what's come to light

Light

The filament of a light bulb is also made from highly resistant material, usually the metal tungsten. As current passes through it, the filament becomes so hot that it glows white, producing light.

Tungsten filament

Glass protects the filament from oxygen, which would destroy it

Wires carrying current

Metal contact joins to electric circuit

Watt is it?

50

Electromagnetism

An electric current flowing through a wire produces a magnetic field around the wire. When the current is switched off, the magnetic field disappears. The bigger the current and the more wire there is, the stronger the electromagnet's magnetic force.

South pole
Magnetic field
North pole
Flow of current
Coil
Battery

Electromagnets at work

Lots of scrap metal can be moved easily using giant electromagnets. The current is turned on to pick up and transport the load, then turned off to shut off the magnetic field, releasing the metal in a new location.

Drop!

Motor

In a motor, a current passes through a wire coil in one direction and then the other, creating a changing magnetic field. Magnets on either side of the wire alternately attract and repel the coil, forcing it to turn. This energy can be harnessed to power machines.

Magnetic field
Commutator reverses the flow of current each half turn, reversing the coil's poles
Coil
Direction of current
Battery

Generator

When a coil of wire is turned inside a magnetic field or a magnet is moved past a stationery wire, an electric current passes through the wire. A generator uses this effect to create current from movement, the opposite principle from how a motor works.

Coil
Magnetic field
Commutator
Magnet
Bulb lights up when handle is turned
Direction of current flow
Handle turns coil

Michael Faraday

English scientist Michael Faraday (1791–1867) proved that magnetism could produce electricity by pushing a magnet in and out of a coil of wire to create a current. He invented the electric motor and a basic generator.

Clap hands for Hans!

Hans Christian Ørsted

Danish scientist Hans Christian Ørsted (1777–1851) discovered the link between magnetism and electricity when he noticed that turning a current on and off made the needle of a nearby compass jump.

Electricity supply

The electric energy we use is supplied by power plants, and is brought to us via a system of metal cables carried by pylons. When the cables reach city streets, they are usually run underground to deliver electricity to buildings.

Power plant

Most of our electricity comes from fossil fuels, such as coal, oil, and gas. These are burned to heat water, which in turn drives spinning blades called turbines inside massive generators to produce electricity. Nuclear energy—the harnessing of the energy inside an atom's nucleus—can also be used to make electricity.

Power rangers

I get a real buzz off you

Wire coils wound around inside of the transformer
Outer plastic covering
High voltage flows in
Iron core
Lower voltage flows out

MAINS TRANSFORMER

Transformer

The electrical pressure that drives current is called voltage. Cables carrying current from power plants have a dangerously high voltage. Before electricity arrives in homes and workplaces, a device called a transformer lowers the voltage to make it safer.

Electric chemistry

Just as some chemical reactions need light or heat to make them work, other reactions require electrical energy. Some chemical reactions even create an electric current. Electrochemical reactions are used to extract metals from ores, separate hydrogen from seawater, and produce the portable power source we use every day—the battery.

Electrolysis

The process of passing an electric current through a compound to split it into simpler parts is called electrolysis. When saltwater undergoes electrolysis, it breaks apart to form chlorine gas, hydrogen gas, and sodium hydroxide.

ELECTROLYSIS OF SALTWATER

Power supply

Flow of electrons

Anode (+)

Cathode (−)

Negative chlorine (Cl⁻) ions move to anode

Electrolyte of saltwater (H_2O + $NaCl$)

Positive hydrogen (H⁺) ions move to cathode

Liquid becomes sodium hydroxide ($NaOH$) solution

Electrode

A battery is connected to two electrical conductor rods, called electrodes. Each electrode becomes electrically charged when the circuit is complete. The negatively charged electrode is called the cathode and the positively charged electrode is called the anode.

Positive electrode

Negative electrode

Electrolyte of saltwater (H_2O + $NaCl$)

Chlorine (Cl_2)

Hydrogen (H_2)

Electrolyte

The electrodes are placed in a mixture called an electrolyte, which may be solid or liquid. The electrolyte is a conductor, so the current now has a complete circuit to move around, from the battery to the cathode, across the electrolyte to the anode, and back to the battery.

Hydrogen cars

The gas used to fuel hydrogen cars is often produced by electrolysis of saltwater. Unlike diesel-fueled or gasoline-fueled cars, hydrogen cars produce no harmful emissions. The engine is driven by the reaction of hydrogen with oxygen, producing one simple, clean waste product—water.

Humphrey Davy

In 1807, British scientist Sir Humphrey Davy (1778–1829) built a battery more powerful than any that had existed previously. He used the power to split compounds apart using electrolysis, and discovered many new elements, including potassium, sodium, calcium, magnesium, boron, and barium.

Electroplating

Cheap metal can be given a coat of shiny, expensive metal by electrolysis. The cheap object is used as the cathode and a sheet of the expensive metal is the anode. The electrolyte also contains a compound of the anode metal. As the current flows, metal moves into the solution from the anode, wearing it away, then from the solution to form a layer on the cathode.

ELECTROPLATING A TROPHY

Battery — Current

Gold anode (+)

Cup cathode (−)

Ready for a worthy winner

Who needs batteries?

Congratulations!

Cheers!

Speed demons!

How a battery works

Electrolysis turns electrical energy into chemical energy, but a battery does the opposite, turning chemical energy into electrical energy. Inside the battery, the compound used as an electrolyte reacts with each electrode. The reactions make one electrode lose electrons and the other electrode gain them, producing a current when the battery is connected to a circuit.

INSIDE A BATTERY

Light bulb

Current

Current

Current

Current

Battery has a positive cathode—graphite (+)

Electrolyte paste

Battery has a negative anode—zinc (−)

Current

Rowdy bunch

Lap the cheetah!

Terminals

A battery's electrodes are called terminals. In a battery with a solid electrolyte, called a dry battery, the cathode is the graphite rod in the center, and the battery case is the anode.

Rockets are not in the rules

Take a spin?

No thanks

Who cares about rules?

Alessandro Volta

In 1800, Italian Alessandro Volta (1745–1827), invented the battery, using zinc and copper disks as electrodes, and cardboard soaked in saltwater as the electrolyte. Sets of disks were stacked to produce more electricity, giving the battery its original name, the "Voltaic pile."

Volta is numero uno

Rechargeable battery

Some batteries stop working when all the chemicals inside them are used up and the reactions stop. With rechargeable batteries, applying an electric current reverses the reactions, so the battery can be used again.

Battery needs recharging

Let's cut a deal

It's the pits

Road hog!

Car batteries

The electric current needed to start a car engine is provided by the car's huge acid-filled rechargeable battery. As the car moves, its motion powers a generator called an alternator inside the engine, which produces electricity to recharge the battery.

CAR BATTERY

Lead oxide electrode

Pure lead electrode

Sulfuric acid (electrolyte)

FINISH

53

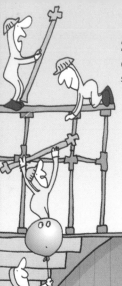

Simultaneous discoveries

Often in the history of science, several scientists have worked on the same problem at the same time, in a race to be the first to make a breakthrough. This has sometimes led to two scientists coming up with a new idea at once, making it impossible to decide who should get the credit for the discovery.

Calculus

In 1675, English physicist Sir Isaac Newton and German physicist Gottfried Leibniz both came up with a mathematical theory called calculus. Newton insisted that Leibniz had stolen his ideas.

This was a calculated act of robbery

I don't know what you mean

Chance discoveries

Most scientific discoveries are the result of years of study and hard work. But from time to time, something unexpected is revealed, which leads to an entirely new discovery. For this reason, scientists always observe every aspect of whatever they are studying, even tiny factors that may seem irrelevant.

Microwave oven

While working with microwave radar signals in 1945, American engineer Percy Lebaron Spencer noticed his candy bar had melted. He double-checked the effect by putting some corn in the path of the beam. He had discovered the principle of the microwave oven!

1939

American scientist Linus Pauling explains the nature of chemical bonds. (*See p.11*)

1930s

Scientists investigate subatomic particles and this leads to the splitting of the atom. The process is explained and called nuclear fission in 1939.

Modern chemistry

Chemists now know how atoms are made and how they bond to create molecules, so they can alter substances by manipulating the atoms and molecules. The alchemists' dream of changing one element into another may yet become a reality.

1911

New Zealand physicist Ernest Rutherford discovers the shape of the atom. (*See p.10*)

1905

German physicist Albert Einstein publishes his theory of special relativity. A decade later, he establishes his theory of general relativity. (*See p.45*)

Alchemy

The study of alchemy spread from ancient China, reaching Europe in the 13th century. Alchemists were searching for the secret to eternal life, and a way to create gold from other metals. These goals seemed impossible, but their experiments led to developments in chemistry and medicine.

Going for gold!

Medieval methods

In the Middle Ages, scientific principles were applied to practical purposes, creating great leaps in technology. The wheelbarrow, the crank (a type of gear), and waterwheels made it possible to construct huge buildings.

1220–25

English philosopher Robert Grosseteste develops the first scientific method. He works with mirrors and lenses on actual experiments, concluding that light is the basic substance in the universe. (*See p.36*)

12th–16th centuries

Gothic cathedrals built in Europe, using scientific principles.

13th century CE

Qutb al-Din al-Shirazi and Kamal al-Din al-Farisi discover why rainbows occur. (*See p.39*)

9th century CE

Ja'far Muhammad ibn Musa ibn Shakir discovers gravitational pull between planets and stars. (*See p.44*)

8th century CE

Ja'far al-Sadiq discovers that tiny particles (atoms) have positive and negative charge. (*See p.10*)

I'm in charge

Islamic ideas

The Arabian Empire spread through western Asia and around the Mediterranean from the 7th century CE. The Arabs' religion, Islam, encouraged the study of medicine, astronomy, and mathematics. Islamic philosophers translated the scientific works of ancient Greece, then began to analyze and improve on their ideas.

BURSTS OF IDEAS

LIBRARY
(please be quiet)

Throughout history, there have been periods when science was considered all-important and great discoveries came thick and fast, as well as times when science was virtually forgotten, with scholars merely accepting the ideas of the past. While science has often been at the forefront of new technology, many inventions were developed long before scientists worked out the principles behind them.

Your books are overdue!

The spread of knowledge

Today, new scientific ideas spread around the world very quickly. However, in the past, there were long periods when one region was much more scientifically advanced than another. This timeline shows the history of science, including revolutionary ideas and discoveries.

The numbers in parentheses indicate the pages to look at to learn more about these groundbreaking ideas.

Getting it wrong

Scientists repeatedly refer back to the work of scientists who have gone before them, reconstructing their experiments to test the ideas and check the evidence. Often a correct scientific idea is only generated when someone realizes that an earlier scientist's ideas are wrong.

Universal change

For 1,500 years, people accepted Greek philosopher Ptolemy's view that the universe revolved around Earth. The 16th-century astronomer Nicolaus Copernicus found flaws in the theory and realized that, in fact, Earth and the other planets of the solar system move around the Sun.

New ideas

For the future of science, one thing is certain. Scientists will continue to expand our existing knowledge with new ideas, fresh theories, and exciting discoveries.

1898

Physicists Marie and Pierre Curie isolate two radioactive elements, radium and polonium.

The new physics

The discovery of radioactivity showed that matter and energy were extremely complex. The new sciences of quantum mechanics and particle physics began to delve into the mysteries of subatomic particles.

1895

German physicist Wilhelm Röntgen produces X-rays.
(See p.39)

1848

Irish scientist William Thomson (Lord Kelvin) discovers the concept of absolute zero.
(See p.34)

1843

The work of English physicist James Prescott Joule leads to the law of conservation of energy.
(See p.31)

19th-century science

In the 19th century, with advances such as the periodic table and the harnessing of electricity and magnetism to create power, science was on the way to quantifying, categorizing, defining, and explaining everything in the universe.

Birth of modern science

During the Renaissance period, European scholars began to question scientific ideas that had been handed down for centuries. Scientists did more than just observe and theorize about the universe: they began to experiment to discover new ways of looking at things.

I'm a Sun worshiper

1543

Polish astronomer Nicolaus Copernicus states that the Sun is the center of the solar system.

1600

English scientist William Gilbert discovers Earth's magnetic field. *(See p.47)*

1676

Danish astronomer Ole Rømer measures the speed of light.
(See p.37)

Roman empire

Scientific investigation slowed down under the Romans. They admired the culture of Greece and studied works by Greek philosophers. However, the Romans made many advances in technology, including the invention of concrete, which they used to construct engineering wonders, such as aqueducts and amphitheaters.

3rd century BCE

Eratosthenes measures the size of Earth and its distance to the Sun and Moon.

Pass the tape measure

5th century BCE

Democritus teaches that atoms are the smallest parts of matter.

His ideas really matter

Ancient Greece

Religion in Ancient Greece did not try to explain how the universe worked, so scholars known as natural philosophers began to investigate for themselves. They believed everything was made from one of four elements: earth, air, fire, and water. Their ideas were based entirely on observations, because they thought experiments created unnatural conditions and unreliable answers.

c. 2200 BCE Stonehenge built in England

I loved rolling those stones

c. 3000 BCE

Mesopotamia numerals first developed and used

c. 2560 BCE

Great Pyramid (also known as Khufu's Pyramid) built at Giza, Egypt

Prehistoric science

Before people had writing or numbers, their understanding of the world came from religion, astronomy, and nature. They managed to construct amazing religious monuments, such as Stonehenge in England.

Ancient world

Astronomy and religion still dominated the ancient cultures of Mesopotamia (around modern Iraq), India, Egypt, and China, but with the invention of numbers, mathematics developed. This enabled people to investigate chemistry and medicine, and develop architecture and new technologies.

Theoretical science

Some of the greatest scientists never conduct a single experiment or make any observations of their own. This branch of science is called "theoretical," since it is concerned with using information that is already available to come up with new scientific theories, and unlock the secrets of our future in the universe.

Making waves

Just as boats produce ripples on water, scientists believe objects in space produce gravitational waves in the structure of space-time. These waves pass unchanged through any material, alternately stretching and shrinking distances. Gravitational wave astronomy can greatly increase our knowledge of the universe.

Wave ripples outward through space

Center of gravity wave

I can stretch higher

The future's bright

I've shrunk!

Do I have time for a bath?

Our destiny

By looking at data about the universe and forces within it, scientists are trying to figure out if it will continue to expand or disintegrate, or even collapse and then be recreated. These possibilities seem to depend on dark matter, so when we understand that, we may know the fate of the universe.

I could be wrong though

The end is nigh

CERN PARTICLE COLLIDER
Particles speed around main ring

Detector measures particle energies

Subatomic particle (proton)

Up and atom

At the CERN particle collider under Geneva, Switzerland, scientists are making subatomic particles crash into each other at close to the speed of light. Among other things, scientists are trying to detect the Higgs boson, a particle that is thought to give other particles mass.

Can I have one?

It's on!

In the dark

More than 96 percent of the universe is made up of invisible matter, which can only be detected by observing its gravitational effect on detectable matter. Scientists have called this dark matter, and it is responsible for both holding visible matter together, and the expansion of the universe.

I can't see it!

Extra elements

Chemists are currently trying to create the synthetic elements needed to complete the periodic table. Most large elements last only seconds before they decay, but scientists believe that certain elements could be stable if synthesized, and so used for new scientific breakthroughs.

Looking deeper, seeing farther

As scientific instruments and techniques become more accurate, scientists can observe the universe in greater detail, looking deeper into particles of atoms and farther into space.

I made it myself

Future science

What will the future look like? It's impossible to know. Just 100 years ago, there were no computers, so no one could predict how important these machines would become. Similarly, 200 years ago, electromagnetic radiation had not been discovered, so no one could imagine the televisions or cell phones that rely on these waves. The only certainty is that scientists will go on discovering new information about the universe, and devise new ways to use science to transform people's lives.

Going up, and up, and up...

I've had enough of the library!

Incredible innovations

Inventors and manufacturers can use the latest scientific ideas to invent new technology, providing practical innovations that will make people's lives easier or more entertaining, such as artificially intelligent robots.

Theory of everything

There are four fundamental forces at work in the universe: gravity, electromagnetism, and the strong and weak nuclear forces that hold atoms together. Quantum theory explains how the last three fit together, but gravity does not seem to fit. Scientists are searching for one theory that will explain how all these forces are connected.

STRONG NUCLEAR FORCE

WEAK NUCLEAR FORCE

ELECTRO-MAGNETISM

GRAVITY

Nearly got it!

Small world

Scientists can now manipulate individual molecules to create new materials and build microscopic machine parts. At present, nanotechnology is mainly used to make specialized fabrics and pharmaceuticals, but eventually it could be used to create tiny engines or robots powered by nanobatteries.

He's so fly!

Union fusion

The solution to the world's energy problems could be nuclear fusion, if scientists discover an economical way to achieve it on a large scale. Today's nuclear power plants use nuclear fission, splitting atoms and producing deadly radioactive waste. Nuclear fusion joins atoms together and produces no dangerous waste.

Toroidal field magnet

Vacuum chamber

Poloidal field magnet

Plasma

NUCLEAR FUSION REACTOR

Cleaner cars

Hydrogen-fuelled cars emit less pollution than most other vehicles, but producing hydrogen uses vast quantities of fossil fuels, which contribute to global warming. Future technology will aim to discover a clean, cheap, and efficient method of producing hydrogen, using renewable sources such as wind or solar power.

Nice wheels

This is going to hurt

Where did y... chute off to... ...ought I m... myself nu-clear!

Time travelers

According to Albert Einstein, it might be possible to time travel back into the past, but it would be impossible to travel into the future. But you never know—scientists have declared lots of things impossible, and then turned out to be wrong.

Past Present Future Time-travel trips

Meet my pet dino

Greetings from the future

Revolutionary robots

Although electronic computers have been around since the mid-20th century, there are still no machines that can compete with the flexibility of the human mind. In the future, the artificial intelligence of computers and robots will develop, enabling them to reason and learn from past experiences, solve problems, understand environments, and use language.

My wheels are killing me!

They're so smart!

SKY CAFÉ

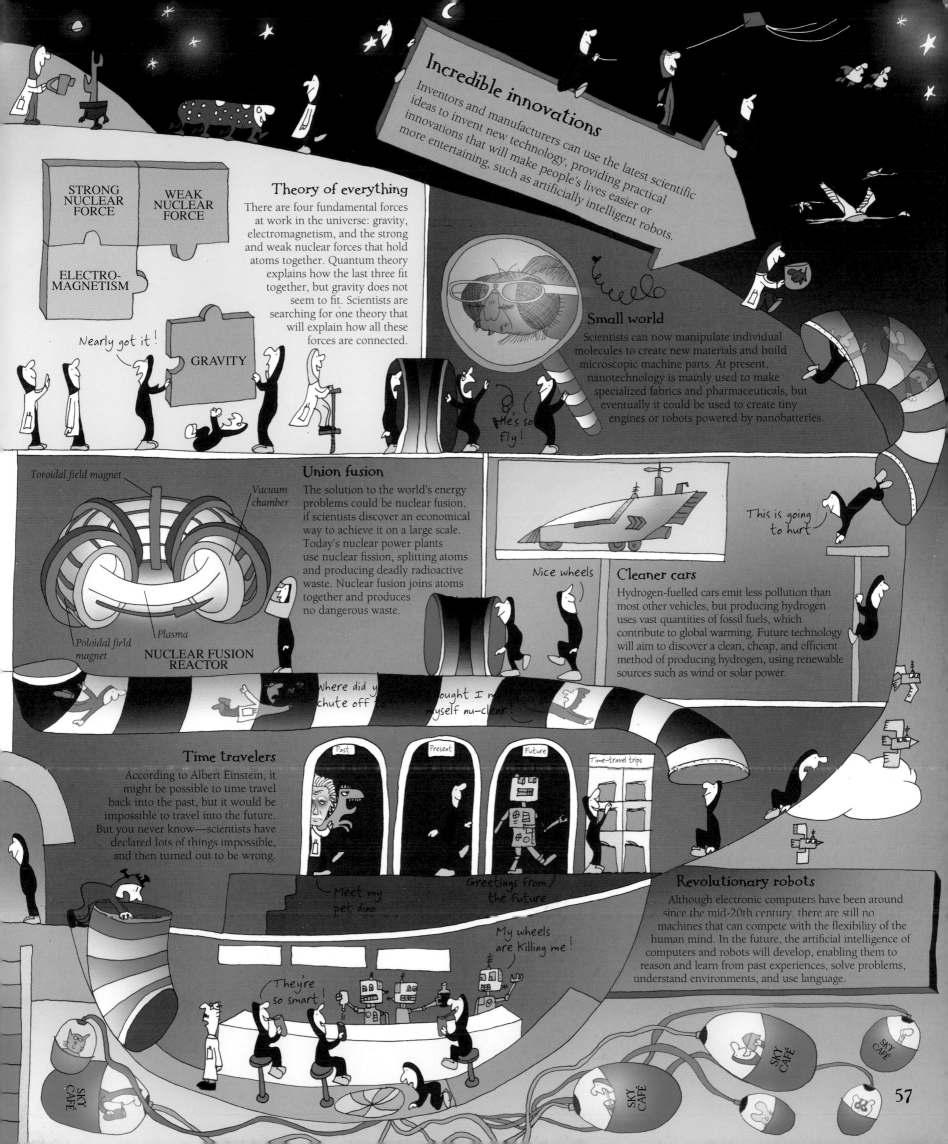

Acid
A compound containing hydrogen that splits up in water to produce positive hydrogen ions. Acids have a pH below 7.

Alkali
A base that dissolves in water, to create negatively charged hydroxide ions (OH^-).

Alloy
A mixture of a metal and another substance.

Amplitude
The maximum height or depth of a wave, measured from a central point.

Astronomy
A branch of science that looks at the universe, planets, and stars.

Atom
The smallest part of an element that can exist and still have the characteristics of that element.

Base
A compound that reacts with acid to form a salt. A base has a pH above 7.

Biology
A branch of science concerned with the structure and behavior of living organisms, such as plants and animals.

Bond
An attraction between atoms that holds them together as molecules.

Botany
The branch of biology concerned with plants.

Catalyst
A substance that speeds up a chemical reaction without itself undergoing any change.

Chemical reaction
A process that changes substances into new substances by breaking and making chemical bonds.

Chemistry
A branch of science concerned with the composition of substances and how they react with each other.

Circuit
A path through which an electric current can flow.

Compound
A substance formed from two or more chemically bonded elements.

Conduction
The process by which heat or electricity passes through a substance.

Conductor
A substance that allows heat or electricity to pass through it easily.

Convection
The transfer of heat through a liquid or gas caused by warmer, less dense material rising, and cooler, more dense material falling.

Crystal
A solid substance with molecules arranged in a regular pattern.

Current
A flow of electrons.

Dissolving
When a substance mixes into another substance completely, with every part of the mixture the same.

Distillation
A process for purifying or separating liquids by first boiling and then cooling the liquid.

Efficiency
A measure of how much energy is turned into useful work by a machine.

Electricity
The effect created by the movement or buildup of electrons.

Electrode
A conductor through which electricity enters or leaves something.

Electrolysis
A chemical reaction created by passing a current through an electrolyte.

Electrolyte
A compound that conducts electricity in electrochemical reactions.

Electromagnetic spectrum
A group of energy-carrying waves arranged in order of increasing wavelength, including radio waves, microwaves, infrared waves, visible light, ultraviolet waves, X-rays, and gamma rays.

Electromagnetism
The relationship between electricity and magnetism.

Electron
A subatomic particle with a negative charge, found in orbits around an atom's nucleus.

Element
A substance that cannot be broken into any simpler substance by physical or chemical means.

Endothermic reaction
A reaction in which heat is taken in.

Energy
The ability of matter and radiation to do work. There are many forms of energy, and the unit for measuring energy is a joule (j).

Equation
A way of using symbols to represent how the reactants of a chemical reaction turn into the products. Each side of the equation must be balanced.

Exothermic reaction
A reaction in which heat is given out.

Experiment
A scientific procedure carried out to test a hypothesis or prove a theory.

Force
A push or a pull that changes the motion of an object. Force is measured in newtons (n).

Frequency
The number of waves passing a point each second, measured in hertz (hz).

Friction
A force caused by one surface rubbing against another.

Fulcrum
The fixed turning point of a lever.

Gas
A state of matter with no definite shape or fixed volume. Molecules in gasses have lots of kinetic energy.

Genetics
The branch of biology concerned with inherited characteristics between generations of plants and animals.

Gravity
The force of attraction between two objects that have mass.

Inertia
An object's resistance to any change in motion.

Inorganic chemistry
A field of chemistry that looks at substances that contain no carbon or only a very tiny amount of carbon.

Insulator
A material that is a poor conductor of heat or electricity.

Ion
An atom or group of atoms that has lost or gained electrons and so become electrically charged.

Kinetic energy
The energy a body has because of its motion.

Law
A statement of a scientific fact that says a certain thing will always happen under certain conditions, for example, Newton's laws of motion.

Lens
A piece of glass or plastic used to refract light. The center of a convex lens curves toward you, and the center of a concave lens bends away from you.

Lever
A simple machine consisting of a rigid bar turning around a fixed point called the fulcrum.

Tow infinity, and beyond!

You've got great definition

Liquid
A state of matter with no definite shape and fixed volume. Molecules in liquids have more kinetic energy than in solids, but less than in gasses.

Load
The load is the object moved or balanced by a machine.

Machine
A device that changes one force into another to make work easier.

Magnetic field
An area around a magnet influenced by the magnet's force.

Mass
The amount of matter in a body.

Mathematics
A branch of science concerned with the measurement, properties, and relationships of quantities and sets, using numbers and symbols.

Matter
Anything that has mass and fills space.

Mechanics
This area of physics looks at motion and the forces that produce it.

Meniscus
The curved surface of a liquid, caused by a variation in surface tension where the liquid touches the container.

Molecule
The smallest unit of an atom or a compound that can exist and still have the properties of that atom or compound, usually made of two or more bonded atoms.

Momentum
An object's tendency to keep moving, measured by multiplying its mass by its velocity.

Natural elements
The 94 elements that make up all the matter on Earth.

Neutral
A substance that is neither acid nor alkaline, such as water.

Neutron
A subatomic particle with no electric charge, found in an atom's nucleus.

Nuclear physics
The branch of physics that studies and splits tiny particles called atoms.

Nuclear reaction
A reaction that splits apart or fuses together atomic nuclei.

Nucleus
The central part of an atom, containing protons and neutrons. The nucleus has a positive charge.

Organic chemistry
A field of chemistry concerned with substances that contain carbon, the substance vital to all living matter.

Peak
The highest point that a wave reaches.

Periodic table
A table of all the elements that exist arranged in order of increasing atomic number. Elements with similar atomic structure are grouped in columns.

Petrochemical
A substance produced from petroleum or natural gas.

pH
The "power of Hydrogen": the measure of how acid or alkaline a substance is.

Pharmaceutical
A manufactured medicinal drug.

Photon
The particle responsible for electromagnetic energy.

Physics
A branch of science concerned with energy and forces. Physics looks at the very small (nuclear physics) to the science of the universe.

Pitch
The high or low quality of a sound produced by its frequency.

Pole
One of the two opposite points on a magnet where the magnetic forces are strongest.

Polymer
A substance made from many identical molecules bonded together to form a long chain.

Potential energy
Energy stored for later use, for example, coal has potential energy, which can be converted to heat energy.

Power
The amount of work carried out in a certain time, measured in watts.

Proton
A subatomic particle with a positive charge found in the nucleus of an atom.

Radiation
Energy traveling as electromagnetic waves, such as light or heat.

Reactant
A substance that takes part in a chemical reaction, and is changed by the reaction.

Refraction
The bending of a beam of light as it passes from one substance into another, for example, from air to glass.

Resistance
The amount that a substance opposes the flow of an electric current.

Solid
A state of matter with a definite shape and fixed volume. Molecules in solids have little kinetic energy.

Solute
A substance that dissolves to form a solution.

Solution
A mixture made by dissolving one substance in another. The molecules of the substances are so evenly mixed that every part of the mixture is the same.

Solvent
A substance that dissolves other substances to form a solution.

Static electricity
An effect caused by electrons building up in one place and creating an electric charge.

Suspension
A mixture containing particles too large to dissolve but light enough to hang or float in the liquid or gas they are mixed with.

Synthetic
Created artificially rather than occurring naturally, for example, all the elements heavier than plutonium are synthetic.

Theory
An idea that explains why something happens as it does, for example, the Theory of Relativity.

Trough
The lowest point that a wave reaches.

Velocity
The speed and direction of an object.

Vibration
A repetitive movement back and forth or up and down.

Visible spectrum
The part of the electromagnetic spectrum that people can see as visible light.

Wavelength
The distance between two equivalent points on neighbouring waves.

Work
The amount of energy needed to perform a task, measured in joules (j).

Zoology
The branch of biology that is concerned with animals.

Let's not gloss over this part

INDEX

Acknowledgments

Dorling Kindersley would like to thank Charlotte Webb for proofreading and Jackie Brind for the index.

No Brainwaves were harmed during the making of this book.